Staying with the Aunts

Hony Family Tree

William Hony, Vicar of Liskeard *m.* (1782) Selina, daughter of George Byam and Louisa (née Bathurst)
d. 1795   b. 1760   d. 1846

| Peter (absentee clergyman) b. 1783 d. 1876 | George (sailor) b. 1784 d. 1812 | Henry (soldier) b. 1788 d. 1809 | | Selina b. 1790 d. 1869 | Henrietta (Harriet) b. 1792 d. 1859 | Caroline b. 1795 d. 1873 |

(6 other children died young)

William Hony *m.* (1827) Margaret Earle
(Fellow of Exeter College)   (daughter of N. Earle
Vicar of Baverstock,   Vicar of Swinford, Oxford)
Archdeacon of Sarum   sister of 'Great Aunt Anne'
b. 1788
d. 1875

| Selina b. 1828 d. 1924 | Margaret b. 1830 d. 1923 | Louisa b. 1832 d. 1905 | Caroline b. 1835 d. 1926 | George b. 1837 d. 1901 | Charles *m.* Annie Lewin b. 1840 d. 1912 | Mary b. 1845 d. 1929 |

2 boys and 5 girls (including the author)

Staying
with the Aunts

IDA GANDY

ILLUSTRATED BY LYNTON LAMB

1989
ALAN SUTTON

TO MY SON CHRISTOPHER
WHOSE CONSTANT ENCOURAGEMENT
HELPED ME TO WRITE
THIS BOOK

ALAN SUTTON PUBLISHING
BRUNSWICK ROAD · GLOUCESTER

First published in 1963 by Harvill Press Limited, London.

This edition published in 1989

British Library Cataloguing in Publication Data

Gandy, Ida
Staying with the aunts.
1. England. Social life, 1910–1936
Biographies
I. Title
942.083′092′4

ISBN 0–86299–589–2

Cover picture: Gathering Flowers *by Royle.*
Photograph: The Bridgeman Art Gallery.

For his Baverstock drawings Mr Lynton Lamb was able to
refer to the hundred-year-old Sketchbooks of one of the
Aunts.

Printed and bound in Great Britain
The Guernsey Press Co. Ltd., Guernsey, Channel Islands.

Contents

Biographical Introduction

Ida Gandy (née Hony) was born in 1885. Her paternal ancestors had been for generations parsons or landowners, often both, first in Cornwall and later in Wiltshire. Her grandfather was a fellow of Exeter College, Oxford, held one of the college livings and later became Archdeacon of Sarum, living partly in the close at Salisbury. He was an enthusiastic botanist, geologist and archaeologist. His son, Ida's father, was vicar of Bishops Cannings near Devizes and later of neighbouring Woodborough. Her mother's family were engineers, builders and timber merchants; Ida's maternal grandfather, Stephen Lewin, was a keen student of church architecture. When only twenty-one he published a book illustrated by himself on Lincolnshire churches; later he submitted a design for the Albert Memorial and designed and made railway engines. Emphatically not the typical parson's wife of the 1880s, his daughter could not sew a button on straight or sing a hymn in tune; she allowed the children to run barefoot and put the girls into serge knickers instead of the then correct white frilly drawers. She frequently entered literary competitions in the newspapers and once won a prize with a review of a play she had never seen.

Her daughter Ida was always a compulsive writer. Another of her enthusiasms was for social reform. After a short semi-academic stay in Oxford with a University family, she set off to undertake social work in London – again, not the conventional choice for a young girl of good family. A job with the Workers' Educational Association took her to Peppard in south Oxfordshire where she met the local GP, Dr Thomas Gandy, whom she married in 1915. He became Chairman of the local Labour Party – even less 'the thing' in those days.

Dr Gandy and his wife stayed in Peppard for fifteen years and had three children. Mrs Gandy began to write and stage plays for the local amateurs, some of which were published and widely performed. She also wrote children's books; her *Three Bold Explorers*, based on the childhood experiences of herself and her siblings, was followed in 1929 by *Sunset Island*, in which legendary supernatural figures – Kelpies, Boggarts, Leprechauns (she had read them all up in the British Museum) – were pictured as surviving together on a distant western island. Then in 1930 came her first well-known book, *A Wiltshire Childhood* (reprinted in 1988 by Alan Sutton Publishing). J.C. Squire published one of her short stories in the *London Mercury*, then the leading literary periodical.

Ida had for years pined for wilder country than the already urbanized landscape of south Oxfordshire and in 1930 she persuaded her husband to move to Clunbury in Shropshire, the surroundings of which provided the background for her next children's book, *Under the Chestnut Tree* (1938). Supported by a cast of villagers from Clunbury she also broadcast from the BBC in Birmingham on Shropshire life.

Bred in the tradition of service to the community cherished by country parsons and doctors, she had long been active in the Women's Institute, and during the Second World War was involved in strenuous work for evacuees and other good causes. In 1945 she and her husband retired to Cerne Abbas in Dorset. He died in 1948 and Mrs Gandy returned to her own county of Wiltshire and settled in Aldbourne near Marl-borough.

Her children long since grown up and away from home (to see them she visited Iran, Portugal, Libya and the USA) and her energies unabated, Ida now resumed writing. In 1960 she published *Round About the Little Steeple*, a carefully research-ed social history of her birthplace, Bishops Cannings, which was followed in 1963 by *Staying with the Aunts*, a vivid account of her father's family and in particular of her five maiden aunts, survivors from the Victorian age, who lived together and kept their coachman and carriage into the 1920s.

Ida was now approaching eighty but still books came. Her passion for the unspoilt Shropshire landscape led in 1970 to *An Idler on the Shropshire Borders*, a nostalgic volume of description and reminiscence. Her last book, *The Heart of a Village*, about the past and present of Aldbourne, where she had lived since 1950, appeared in 1975 – her ninetieth year. She died in September 1977.

I

Arrival at Eling Manor

The strong emotions aroused by the prospect of a visit to the Aunts did not start with the packing of trunks, nor yet with the sandwiching of the family into the old black cab driven by our friend Joliffe from the livery stables in Devizes; nor even with the scramble into the green train itself.

All that belonged equally to our annual holiday in Cornwall. Only when a change from the green Great Western train to the maroon South Western brought us first glimpses of huge ships in Southampton Docks, succeeded by a shining strip of water that narrowed steadily through pale marshland, did these emotions truly begin to stir in us. And when we tumbled out of the train at Redbridge they bubbled like a fountain. For already from the window we had caught sight of the waggonette, and Hazel and Walnut, the fat grey horses, and of Lever, the coachman, sitting motionless behind them.

From the moment we climbed into our seats, sometimes as many as five of us at once, we left behind the uninhibited life of our Wiltshire vicarage—our ramblings, our meals in the garden, our barefooted, happy-go-lucky, untidy ways— and entered the dignified, well-ordered, luxurious, and slightly alarming world of the Aunts. Yet Lever himself, in

9

the tight, green coat with silver buttons (that grew tighter
and shabbier as the years went by), with his broad figure and
his welcoming smile, was an assurance that nothing had
changed, that everything would run true to pattern.

Perhaps I was wrong to say that the Aunts' world began
for us at the station. For they hated with a bitter hatred the
ugly little town through which we must pass; uglier than
ever now, and a mere suburb of Southampton. They
shuddered at each new house, at each added street, as a
creeping menace to their peace. So it was only when the rows
of red-brick dwellings were left behind, and, turning a corner,
we came suddenly to the mill and the Toll Gate, where the
miller, his face and his clothes as thick with flour as a pastry
board, opened the gate for our passage across the last narrow
strip of Southampton Water; it was only then that we properly entered the kingdom of the Aunts. For here, on the
other side of the water (and as surely differentiated in our
Aunts' minds as heaven from hell), were no rows of red-
brick houses, no hideous chapels, no indifferent, or even
hostile, artisans, no irreverent boys, but pretty thatched
cottages, curtseying old women, and outwardly respectful
children. The church presided like a guardian angel over
the seemly landscape from the top of the little hill that
climbed up above the water; wickedness and ugliness had
been left behind at the Toll Gate.

Plop, plop, plop, went the horses' feet on the soft yellow
road, as they carried us along at what seemed a miraculous
speed after the jog-trot of old Rose drawing the Family Ark
away from Bishops Cannings Vicarage.

A fair prospect of wide woodlands enchanted our eyes as
we turned sharply right at the foot of the hill. At home there
were no woods except the little beech clumps that crowned
our hill-tops and a few small boggy copses in the water-

meadows. The next moment, we saw, towering above a mass of rhododendrons, the tall tulip tree, exotic and exciting, that marked the beginning of the Aunts' domain. How sharp was the contrast between it and our sober elms, between the opulent rhododendrons and our sparse thorn hedge!

The gate was set wide open. As we swept through it our hearts began to hammer a little uncomfortably now that the meeting with the Aunts grew imminent. There, round the bend of the drive, was the gracious white house patterned by a magnolia bearing immense creamy blossoms, and there, standing at the foot of the steps was—yes, there was Aunt Louisa, her silver hair shining in the sun, her sharp little nose tip-tilted, her spare figure excessively upright. She was always the most eager to greet us, the most demonstratively affectionate.

Now, as we scrambled out one by one, began the first of those innumerable kisses that would moisten our unwilling faces during ensuing weeks; in Aunt Louisa's case quite uncompromising kisses full on our mouths, so that we felt the soft hairs about her own. Beside Aunt Louisa, Matilda, the parlour-maid, her generous bosom in striking contrast to my Aunt's flatness, with starched cap set on a frizz of black hair, stood ready to open the carriage door and take the rugs from our knees. Her pock-marked cheeks were crumpled in a welcoming smile, and she appeared almost as pleased as Aunt Louisa to see us. But though she too would kiss us later, it would be unfitting for her to do so now. All she did was to murmur: 'Don't forget to wipe your feet, dears.' For the steps ahead were always of a dazzling whiteness. Half way up them waited the two youngest Aunts— Caroline, broad-hipped, capable, wise, with fine features and hair scraped tightly back above a high forehead, and Mary, still at fifty the baby of the family to her sisters, alwaysa little more frivolously dressed and coiffured than they, and, in our early years at all events, still inclined to be a little arch.

Aunt Selina, the eldest aunt, stood at the entrance of the long hall, a small taut figure in close-fitting dark clothes, with smooth black hair, a slight squint, and prominent teeth over which she buttoned her lips with difficulty. They rarely smiled and when on such an occasion as this they did, one received the impression that they were responding to an order rather than acting on their own.

Even as we tried to reply suitably to her hope that we had had a good journey, a soft sigh and a fluttering behind us announced the approach of her special antipathy, Aunt Margaret.

Always a little late for everything, she drifted now towards us from the shadowy end of the hall, her black lace cap slightly awry on her tow-coloured hair. She was taller than the rest and as we looked at her over Aunt Selina's shoulder she seemed, with her vague clothes and her slight stoop, like a willow tree beside a primly pollarded box bush.

'Dear children,' she breathed, 'so once again summer brings you here,' and she bent to kiss our cheeks, but so lightly that I never quite knew whether her mouth had actually touched me.

Aunt Selina gave one of the snorts indicative of her complete contempt for her sister's way of expressing herself and disappeared abruptly. Aunt Margaret's small beady eyes were turned on us searchingly. 'You look very well, dears. What stout legs you have! You take after your mother in that respect.'

She never failed to refer to our legs. Hers were always hidden under her long clinging skirts, except when she caught them up out of the mud and revealed a pair of black sticks. But now Aunt Louisa, looming in the background, indicated that it was time for her to take charge of us.

In my earliest memories, when I was about six years old, there was yet one other most important person to meet, and that was my grandmother. Aunt Louisa would lead us, perhaps upstairs, perhaps to the Blue Room, and there seated in an armchair we would see a very old lady. A voluminous cap of ruched white tulle framed a kind but remarkably ugly face, with long upper lip, tusk-like teeth and narrow slits for eyes. We were never allowed to stand beside her for more than a minute or two for fear of tiring her. In those, her last years, the energies and solicitude of all five Aunts were unceasingly directed to sparing her the slightest effort, to shielding her from draughts, to watching over every mouthful she swallowed. If she refused her soup an Aunt would gently but firmly spoon it into her mouth heedless of her feeble protests, and it seemed to us that someone was always gliding from the room to fetch her an extra wrap. Yet in spite of these suffocating attentions she was allowed on her ninetieth birthday to drive to Netley Abbey, beside Southampton Water, and sketch the ruins. Framed in a deep gold frame almost as large as itself, the result hung in the drawing-room and was one of the Aunts' most treasured possessions.

But this encounter with my grandmother can only have occurred once or twice. In subsequent memories she does not appear, and after we had said how-d'ye-do to Aunt Margaret, Aunt Louisa would sweep us up the stairs, covered with an immaculate holland drugget, to brush our hair and wash our hands. Elizabeth, the housemaid, came to help in the cleaning process. She was thinner, sharper, more humorous than Matilda; her eyes perpetually twinkled behind her spectacles and when the Aunts bickered or were being particularly old-maidish she even dared to be slightly caustic at their expense. I think she felt a weakness for us, but she was more bracing and less demonstrative than Matilda.

Aunt Louisa took us downstairs again for tea, served on the verandah if the weather was suitable. And, as in all happy memories, the sun seemed invariably to shine on the day of our arrival at Eling Manor.

The verandah approximated to my idea of Paradise, so much did I love it. So vivid is every detail that sometimes I still pace it in my dreams, feel the hot sunshine stream through the glass roof, smell the myrtle trees against the wall, peep through the french windows of the great drawing-room at the huge, slightly awe-inspiring portrait by Gainsborough of my great-grandmother and her parents, at the chandeliers and gilt chairs gleaming from the shadows; or stare between the slender white pillars at a lawn, so much greener and smoother than ours at home, that stretched away to a background of oak trees and rhododendrons. The lawn was set about with cunningly shaped little flower-beds that

still glow in my mind like the patterns made by a kaleido-
scope—so gay were they with brilliant, unaccustomed
flowers, with calceolarias dropping tiny orange balloons,
with rose and lemon begonias, with the startling red, white
and blue of geranium, alyssum, and lobelia, shouting aloud
to be jumped over. Only that was strictly forbidden.

Once that peaceful lawn and all those prim flower-beds
were the scene of terrible havoc. My younger brother, by
leaving a gate open, had let in a herd of cows. They churned
their way across the gravel and in ecstasy made for the
greenness beyond.

An Aunt, peering from her bedroom window, gave the
alarm. All five hurried into the garden, and advanced
towards the cows, shaking their skirts, wringing their hands,
crying contrary directions to each other. The cows, excited
by the strange figures closing in on them, plunged ever
deeper into the soft turf and the beds. The flowers fell before
them, particularly the poor flat-faced stupid begonias. Aunt
Margaret, who had retreated to a safe distance, wept aloud
and tugged at her dress so violently that a petticoat fell to the
ground. Of course it was Aunt Caroline who took control
both of the cows and of her sisters. Her shouts brought
White, the gardener, trotting to her help, and eventually the
marauders were driven out. It was a long time, however,
before my brother heard the last of that episode, and when
he went away the customary tip was withheld.

But the cows in the garden have led me astray from tea on
the verandah. There it was awaiting us now. We knew well
all the ritual that preceded it, with Matilda bustling round
and the Aunts giving vague assistance. The seats along the
wall would have had their cushions turned right way up; the
pink and blue striped cotton rugs from Italy brought out
and stretched over the stone floors to protect auntly legs from

a chill. Little tables from the Blue Room would be covered with lace cloths before the tea-tray, the thin bread and butter, the hot scones, the perennial seed-cake, arrived. We children were slow to discard the idea that Aunts should be waited on. It only gradually dawned on us that Aunts who were definitely a little greedy, as we perceived ours to be, preferred to help themselves.

Particularly was this true of Aunt Margaret. She liked to be thought an ethereal being without any of the grosser instincts. When she let her plate go up for a second helping of roast beef at dinner it was always after this style: 'The merest morsel, dear Caroline. You know what my appetite is like.' Aunt Caroline never betrayed her knowledge by an ironical reply. She merely returned her an ample plateful. So at tea-time Aunt Margaret loved to wander round the little tables and, when everyone seemed fully occupied, to pounce on another scone or to lay two slices of bread and butter so deftly together that you were never sure your eyes had not deceived you.

As for ourselves, on that first afternoon at any rate, we were too anxious to tour the garden to want to linger over tea. But here there were conventions not always observed at home. Not till the last Aunt had swallowed her last drop of tea, or munched her last bit of seed-cake, was it thinkable to get to one's feet. And when we did Aunt Louisa rose quickly too. She was not going to allow us to run away by ourselves, however much we wanted to. We imagined, of course, that she came to see we did none of the forbidden things, such as leaving gates open or helping ourselves to fruit. What we never understood in those days was that she came because it warmed her old heart to watch our enjoyment. And anyway without her we could not have entered the Round House. The Round House stood under a great cedar tree which cast so deep a shadow over it that it was always twilight inside. This, combined with the panes of coloured glass that filled the windows, lent it an almost sacred atmosphere. It was difficult at first not to speak in lowered voices, not to tread softly among the treasures piled within. The croquet set was the crown of them all. Such a grand set it seemed to us. Here, instead of our own small chipped mallets, were some of colossal size, brilliantly varnished, flawless; hoops not bent and rusty but straight and true and immaculately white. Here were balls that never lost their bright tints. Here too was a game played with some rainbow-coloured balls in a way that I have completely forgotten, except that you drove them one by one into a red box with sloping sides. The mere sight of them was intoxicating.

There was other apparatus in the Round House but those two, the croquet set and the rainbow balls, are what I remember best. If we tried to persuade Aunt Louisa to let us play with one of them straight away she would be sure to find an excuse. She liked to spin out our treats as much as she could —to leave us always with something to look forward to next day. Her most usual method of evasion was to say that after our long railway journey we must take things quietly. By the Aunts all journeys were considered excessively tiring. Besides, she would remind us, we had not been round the garden yet, nor the stables. The stables! No sooner had she named them than we were dashing along the path to that enclosed stone courtyard, warm with sunlight, rich with horse scent, where Lever reigned supreme. Here at this moment he was giving Walnut and Hazel a last rub-down before their evening meal, to the accompaniment of that delicious noise, half hissing, half humming, that goes with good grooming.

Inside the stables there lived a dashing bay mare who drew

the dog-cart, and always there was Tommy, the stout white pony, kept especially for us and recently brought in from the field. His character was as solid as his person. Unlike Tavy, our own demon Dartmoor pony, he was an absolute gentleman, as predictable as a Sunday dinner. *He* would never come galloping home leaving our prostrate bodies on the ground. We patted his firm flanks and immediately foresaw ourselves trotting along smooth paths in the Manor woods.

In the walled kitchen garden another delight awaited us. Here under a net grew the most colossal gooseberries I have ever met. Green, red, yellow, they were of surpassing sweetness. In Aunt Louisa's company we were sure of our feast, provided always we spat out the skins. To swallow them was in her eyes both rude and dangerous. But if no Aunt was with us we knew that we must beware of White. There he was now, watching us with a twinkle half humorous, half challenging, as much as to say: 'All right, young 'uns. But wait till I catch you sneaking in here by yourselves!' With his moss-green coat and his chin covered by hair the colour of faded moss, he always seemed to have grown straight out of the earth himself. This made him painfully invisible. Once I remember creeping through the garden door, pausing to make sure I was alone, stealing towards the gooseberries, raising the net—and then without warning something that had been only a small round bush reared up and turned into White. And because White, when no Aunt was present, was a formidable person, I fled without a gooseberry.

On one side of the kitchen garden a field sloped to a small stream. But unfortunately a row of iron palings intervened, and beyond them we were forbidden to go. That would be trespassing. And 'Thou shalt not trespass' was the Aunts' eleventh commandment. A wealth of young frogs hopping about on the banks of the stream made the prohibition particularly maddening. Sometimes we surreptitiously climbed the palings, but always carrying a load of guilt such as never weighed on us when we trespassed at home. The huge composite conscience of the Aunts seemed somehow to possess us too when we stayed with them.

On this first evening we merely sent a fleeting glance towards the stream and passed demurely with Aunt Louisa along the gravel path that bordered the wide tree-grown sweep of grassland. Here was another huge hedge of rhododendrons. Much as I grew to hate them in later years when they appeared in woods that I had imagined were wild, they seemed to occupy their rightful place in the Aunts' garden. I never loved, but I tolerated them there. Now, in the gathering twilight, we poked our heads into their dark recesses and woke the protest of a scurry of blackbirds unused to such invasion of their privacy. A slight dew made Aunt Louisa

insist that we keep to the path. Dew was dangerous and must always be met with goloshes.

There was only one bit of the garden left to explore, and this was the Wilderness. It lay east of the long carriage-drive to the stables, a dense tangle of ancient trees and under-growth dropping to a small damp ravine. We loved it as a place where we could do as we pleased without fear of an Aunt's watchful eye. For the Aunts did not care for the Wilderness. Its dampness and wildness offended them.

So Aunt Louisa let us take the path through it alone, and once more I drank in the gloom and sadness that made a special appeal to the morbid side of my nature.

Anything might have happened here; young men may have hung themselves for love, misunderstood children (of whom I sometimes accounted myself one) may have sorrowed in the bottom of the ravine till they died from exposure. But the sight of Aunt Louisa advancing, brisk and businesslike, to meet us at the other end, quickly dispelled all such non-sense.

Then, in the little room known as the Servants' Hall, glasses of milk and biscuits awaited us. Here there always hung a unique, unforgettable smell due, I suppose, to the big store cupboard from which Aunt Caroline dispensed tea, sugar, dried fruit and spices year after year. Here the maids mended household linen, here on wet days we played battle-dore and shuttlecock. And this was the only room in the house where my father was allowed to smoke his pipe.

Our supper over, Aunt Louisa marshalled us up to bed. The mahogany-encased bath presented another of those sharp contrasts to our home life. There we had little tin tubs full of cold chalk-hard water into which we squeezed with difficulty. Here was an astounding depth and breadth of pale brown water, as hot as Aunt Louisa would allow, soft as silk

21

to the skin, where the soap frothed miraculously. We always longed for the day when we might plunge about in it to our hearts' content, but this was impossible because an Aunt invariably hovered to see that we did not splash the polished woodwork.

Another awe-inspiring place was the water-closet at the end of the passage. Once safely inside it—and Aunt Louisa always reconnoitred to make sure we did not collide with any other Aunt about to enter or to leave it—one climbed up two steps to a mahogany throne as highly polished as the bath. So formidable did this structure seem that during the first day or two our normal bodily functions were often thrown completely out of gear.

Opening into the bathroom was a vast room with a four-poster bed hung with curtains of thick cream damask embroidered in red. Into it my elder sister and I climbed on our first evening with a fluttering of the heart. Then Aunt Louisa closed the window—night air was dangerous, she said—folded the shutters, drew the curtains, bestowed another of her uncompromising kisses, put out the candle on the dressing-table, and left us in the great dark room.

But not for long was it to remain dark. Though in many matters we submitted meekly to her rule, we could not and would not sleep all closed up. When a safe interval had passed one of us would slip from the bed and with utmost caution draw back the curtains a little, unbolt the shutters— a tricky business that—and push up the window. Through it would come not only the warm moist leafy smell that belonged so particularly to the Aunts' garden, not only the call of the owls from the woods and the Wilderness, but sometimes in the early morning another, stranger and more thrilling sound. This was the deep boom of a fog-horn on Southampton Water. Hearing it, I trembled with delicious excitement. It seemed so close at hand that I imagined great ships lost in the fog only just beyond the Toll Gate. I did not want any of them to be actually shipwrecked but it enchanted me to feel danger in the air.

II

My Five Aunts

Aunt Selina, though head of the family, never took the lead in anything. She was excessively retiring and reserved: nobody, not even her own sisters, knew her intimately.

Like a mole she burrowed her way down a dark passage to her own small room and there spent much of the day. How she passed the time nobody ever knew, for she had no artistic gifts, nor did she embroider endless cushion-covers and tea-cosies like Aunt Caroline and Aunt Mary. I think perhaps that letter-writing was her chief occupation, for though her friends were few she kept up with numerous cousins. The letters they received must have been indescribably dull.

There would also have been considerable correspondence with various church societies, since she was very religious— in an Old Testament fashion. 'Thou shalt not' held a prominent place in her make-up, and one received the impression when she read family prayers that she was trying to beat down strong barriers between herself and God.

Emotion, or the show of it at all events, was abhorrent to her, and so was any ardent expression of ideas or feeling. This it was that so continually led to strained relations between herself and Aunt Margaret. She was a bit of dry, condensed prose set alongside a rambling sentimental poem.

In politics she was the most rigidly Conservative of all the five Aunts, and as a Grand Dame of the Primrose League

dutifully took the chair at certain local meetings. Never could
any chairman have been less disposed to open a discussion,
or readier to close it.

When staying at Eling we saw very little of her, and if
she opened her mouth at all, which was not often, it was
usually with an admonition of some sort. Great was our
astonishment, therefore, when one evening, soon after she
had arrived to stay with us at Bishops Cannings, she appeared in the nursery before bedtime and announced that she
had come to have a game with us.

A game! This buttoned-up little Aunt, more than sixty
years old, play a game! We stood transfixed. But Aunt
Selina, undaunted, proceeded in a most businesslike fashion
to teach us 'Lubey Loo':

> Here we come Lubey Loo,
> Here we come Lubey Lout,
> You puts your right foot in,
> You puts your left foot out—

I and my two sisters struggled awkwardly to make our
own feet follow the motions of the ones that darted out from
under her long black skirt. The climax came when she
suddenly lifted one high in the air, crying:

> Shake it a little, a little, a little,
> And turn yourself about!

And with that she spun round like a teetotum.

Then her lips unclosed themselves from over her prominent teeth and she broke into a strange cackle of laughter
—the only one we had ever heard from her.

It was a revelation to us. Unfortunately my mother chose
that moment to open the door and peep in. Her eyes grew
round with surprise.

'Why, Linnie, how kind of you to play with the children!'
she said. Aunt Selina looked like one detected in a crime.
She shut her mouth with a snap, smoothed her black hair,
and said: 'Not at all. It was just an old game we played when
I was young,' and straight away hurried from the room.

She never repeated the performance, but for the first time
we realized that once she had actually been young like ourselves—she of all the Aunts! It was astonishing. Henceforth
'Lubey Loo' is for ever knit up with a taut little figure waving
her leg in the air with complete abandon. For a few happy
moments she had shaken off the years and returned to her
nursery at Baverstock.

When we were quite young Aunt Margaret was perhaps
our most popular Aunt. She seldom interfered with us, rarely
issued an order. We never guessed that this was because she
was too self-absorbed to bother, and that probably she cared
less about us than any other Aunt, except possibly Aunt
Selina. She amused us, even sometimes touched us, with her
poetic fancies. We felt grieved on her behalf when Aunt
Selina and Aunt Louisa sat heavily on her as was their
custom. Particularly were they prone to do so at breakfast
when she enlarged on what she had seen from her window.
All her life she had been passionately interested in the
heavens and sometimes it seemed that she must have been up
half the night gazing at the stars, so much had she to tell
about their individual beauties.

'Dear sisters,' I remember her saying once, 'you should
have seen Venus at five o'clock, glimmering through the
tulip tree. She was so exquisite that I sat in my nightgown
beside the open window, unable to move my eyes from her
till she dissolved in the sunrise.'

At this Aunt Selina's mouth twitched violently.

'Really, Margie, I never heard such nonsense! Sitting by

an open window in your nightgown! Venus indeed! If you start your bronchitis again you will have only yourself to blame!' Her voice trembled with suppressed fury.

Aunt Louisa from the other side of the table observed sourly: 'Up at five o'clock to look at Venus—yet late for prayers as usual!'

A soft sigh, and a turning to Aunt Caroline for sympathy, was Aunt Margaret's invariable reaction to such remarks. She was a sigh embodied. She sighed over Venus and the new moon, over tender memories, over the ugliness beyond the Toll Gate, and the things that the vicar did or left undone. But it would be a mistake to think that her sighs over the rude assaults of her sisters meant a meek acceptance of defeat. Though sometimes she might resemble a willow tree bending and sighing before an icy wind, she could also be tough, could with apparent guilelessness let fall a few words calculated to rouse rage in Aunt Selina, and answer Aunt Louisa in honeyed tones that held a sharp sting bedded in them.

And sometimes—more frequently as she grew older—she would work herself up into a frenzy. Some trifle would serve to open the flood-gates, and then such a torrent of indignation and emotion, fed by a thousand pent-up grievances, would burst out of her that her sisters, even patient Aunt Caroline, would lock themselves into their rooms. From the maids the news would spread to garden and coach-house: 'Miss Margaret is in one of her moods!' Then White and the under-gardener and Beech would hide themselves among the fruit trees, or in the Round House or the harness-room, till all danger of an encounter was over.

For when her sisters had fled from her she would wander distraught into the garden like a female Ancient Mariner in

search of someone to listen to her. Once White, caught un-
awares, was immediately immersed in the flood.

'But what you are saying has nothing to do with me, Miss
Margaret,' he protested. 'And I'm very busy. The greenhouse door is open.'

'Give me five minutes, White—just five minutes,' she
entreated tearfully.

'Five minutes then, miss,' said White and drew out his
watch.

The spate of grievances poured on with no sign of abate-
ment, and White, replacing his watch, said firmly: 'The five
minutes are up. I must go.'

'You have dared to time me!' Aunt Margaret's voice
shook with anger and grief, and away she hurried to tell
Aunt Carry of the insolence to which she had been sub-
jected.

A few minutes later Aunt Caroline sought White in the
greenhouse. 'Oh, White, you shouldn't have done it!' But
she was laughing.

The experience proved salutary. It was a long time before the performance was repeated, and never with White as victim. We children knew nothing of these strange attacks. It was White's daughter who told me the story long afterwards. Aunt Margaret was always very kind to her and her sister, and contrived her own special ways of pleasing them. When all the Aunts went abroad and White and his family moved in to guard the house, she left out various discarded tea-gowns for the children's amusement. Once when they were sweeping along the drive in all their glory a simple old soul from a neighbouring cottage saw them through the gate and dropped a curtsey. They sat on the front steps shaking with laughter for over an hour afterwards.

Aunt Margaret herself loved 'dressing-up', and her general appearance was unlike that of any other Aunt. Besides softly clinging draperies and bits of lace here, there, and everywhere, her ornaments were such as to delight a child's heart. In particular I remember a necklace of ruby-coloured glass beads cut like flowers, which she wore both to please us and herself. Her flat lace cap kept her toupee of false hair in place—or so we referred to it among ourselves, though probably it had been fashioned from her own carefully preserved combings.

Once a terrible thing happened to this toupee. Jock, the black-and-white Pomeranian, loved to lay hold of a variety of objects as playthings, and Aunt Margaret would laugh gently when it was something belonging to Aunt Louisa or Aunt Selina.

One day he was prancing about with what she fancied to be a ball of wool. Suddenly misgiving seized her. She clapped her hand to her head and found it strangely bare. The laughter stopped abruptly.

Because invitations to Aunt Margaret's room were rare

we felt deeply honoured when they came. It was very much *her* room. Of course it faced east; she could have borne no other aspect. Her bed, drawn close under the window, was turned into a divan and covered with a striped Italian rug. Up here she kept her baby grand piano, and entranced others besides ourselves with her playing. Occasionally, especially if she felt compunction about her behaviour towards him, she would beg White to come and listen to her. The under-gardener was never invited, but he might be given a pair of new boots in similar circumstances.

Her special parish activity was the Girls' Friendly Society. The meetings started in the Servants' Hall with minute and careful searching of the scriptures for repetitions of some particular word or phrase. This uninspired teaching was often followed by an eager talk about the stars, the planets, the Milky Way—all the mystery and beauty of the heavens. And sometimes the girls were led up the back staircase for the privilege of a peep into her room and to hear a few chords and ripplings on the piano.

Some of her own sketches and of her mother's hung on the walls. On the chimney-piece stood a variety of objects collected from abroad—bits of Venetian glass, a plate from Brittany, a cloisonné box, and in the centre a turquoise blue Chinese clock ornamented with golden dragons which roused our special admiration. Her bookshelves were stacked with the works of Ruskin, who came next to the Bible in her esteem. As we grew a little older she loved to take down a volume and read aloud a favourite passage. There was Dante too. She fancied the sound of her own Italian and would dwell on the words in unmistakable ecstasy. Though they meant nothing to us we were fascinated by their melody, and by the sway of her long thin body. At such times I believe she drew real satisfaction from our presence. Safe in her own citadel from the darts of Aunt Selina and Aunt Louisa, she could let herself go as much as she pleased without fear of ridicule.

She had, too, a sense of humour pleasing to us children, could say nonsensical things that woke an answering chord in us, joke gently at herself and allow us to laugh with, but never at, her.

The ostensible object of our visit, however, was not to hear her read aloud or to listen to her whimsical sayings, but to drink mid-morning tea from delicate little white and gold cups, and to play on a musical instrument kept specially for us—a xylophone whose notes, tapped out with small ivory hammers, seemed to us of entrancing sweetness. Altogether the impression left by a visit to Aunt Margaret's room was of something rarefied and beautiful, which was just what she intended.

Sometimes these tea-parties took place in the early morning, but then the atmosphere was bound to be less leisurely, and there were arch allusions to what Aunt Louisa might say if 'poor Aunt Maudie' (as she liked to call herself) were late again.

Though most of the Aunts had at one time filled innumerable sketch-books, Aunt Margaret was the only real artist in the family, and hence had been allotted a studio in a quiet corner of the house. To it she retired every morning after that long mysterious interlude in the bedroom common to all the Aunts. I never remember seeing her sketch out of doors, though in her younger days she must often have done so.

In the studio, stacked on the floor, round the walls, on top of cupboards, inside cupboards, were a legion of canvases, some hardly begun, some half or three-quarters finished, a few—very few—complete. Nor was this disproportion due to the departure of completed pictures into the outside world.

Here she also kept her harp.

Aunt Margaret never sold a picture; she would have judged that a shocking breach of taste for one in her position, and she rarely gave one away. Her sense of possession was too strong. Nor, I think, did this multiplicity of wasted canvases ever grieve her. It satisfied her to have spent blissful hours, to have expressed herself, to retain numerous reminders of radiant moments.

Among all these works, finished or unfinished, Salisbury as a subject filled by far the most important place—the quiet, dignified Salisbury of small personal shops and slow-moving horse traffic that existed before the army invaded the Plain. This was the Salisbury to which the family drove each year from Baverstock, their childhood home. Throughout their lives it remained their Mecca, even when awful changes in the early part of the century cut them to the heart, and caused Aunt Margaret to sigh her soul away.

After Salisbury and Baverstock she loved most the New Forest, on the edge of which she and her mother and sisters lived before they moved to Eling. She drew the trees with as much loving care as though her revered Ruskin had looked over her shoulder as she worked. The branches really grew from the trunks. Their growth and foliage made them instantly recognizable as oak or ash, elm or beech. The trees of modern artists, had she lived to see them, would have completely prostrated her. 'Autumn in the Forest' was her favourite theme, and she exquisitely portrayed the mellow tones, the carpet of dead leaves, the woodland paths disappearing under an arch of overhanging boughs.

Since the Aunts were great travellers and went abroad every year till old age tied them down, there was a wealth of sketches, more or less finished, of Italy and the Riviera. In these the colours flowed riotously from her brush. Whole tubes of rose madder, cobalt and ultramarine must have vanished within a week. As she turned the leaves or drew out pictures from the piles on the floor, she loved to roll out the Italian names of the places they represented: Firenze and Fiesole, Bordighera, Rapallo.

They flowed from her tongue with a wealth of pregnant sighs and ejaculations. Humbug though she often was, there could be no doubt that a genuine passion for Italy inspired her.

But among all the contents of the studio by far the most outstanding, in her own eyes at all events, was a large picture that always stood on an easel in the middle of the room, and on which, for as long as I can remember, she never stopped working.

The subject was a sunrise over the sea at Sark, and was called 'The Wings of the Morning'. Year after year she continued to add to it in some way we never understood. Perhaps she increased the number of the ripples on the water or deepened the crimson flush along the horizon. I don't know.

At the beginning of each visit we were invited to call on her in her studio, her manner clearly implying that we must consider ourselves extremely privileged people. Shyly and gravely we entered and allowed ourselves to be placed in the right position for appreciating the great work. Tongue-tied and baffled we stood there, unable to see any change since we had last looked at it, unable to think of any suitable remark, till Aunt Margaret would turn away with a sigh and a gentle insinuation that the artistic strain in her family had not, she feared, been transmitted to us.

Year after year 'The Wings of the Morning' continued to

provide her with occupation and also with a perpetual subject for conversation.

'Dear Carrie,' she would say as she sat down to lunch with an air of pleasant exhaustion, 'it has been a wonderful morning for me. As I painted I saw that sunrise again in all its glory. And now I am tired but satisfied.' Or, with a deep sigh: 'I don't know why but "The Wings of the Morning" eluded me today.'

Aunt Caroline always contrived a sympathetic answer, but on the opposite side of the table an exasperated snort would escape Aunt Selina, and a snapping comment or a loud sniff, Aunt Louisa. Aunt Margaret either turned a deaf ear to both or answered with her customary sigh.

On the days when inspiration failed she might be seen wandering about the rose-garden in a floppy hat with a deep black veil fluttering down behind, while she snipped off dead roses and looked unusually bent and forlorn. What would have happened had she ever truly finished 'The Wings of the Morning' it is impossible to guess. But the sad truth must be told. What started, I think, as a genuine inspiration, with a certain ethereal quality in the upward-sweeping clouds, became at last a heavy, lifeless picture that could never be finished because the initial impetus had run out long ago. And so it was with Aunt Margaret herself.

Though genuinely gifted, her amateurishness, her lack of purpose, resulted in a very small actual achievement. If only her parents had sent her to an art school; if only she had possessed a smaller personal income; if only she had been unfettered by absurd ideas as to what was proper for someone in her position—if only—but there it was.

She was content to be an 'elegant female', working when she pleased, either throwing aside a picture when she was tired of it, or over-elaborating it for want of something better

to do. Even so, if she had retained the qualities that endeared her to us in our early days her old age would not have been the arid thing that it became. But sad to tell, just as the sunrise in her picture lost its glow and the sea its limpidity, so did Aunt Margaret change slowly but persistently into a spiteful, self-indulgent old woman, who never lost an opportunity to denigrate everybody, including her nieces, who failed to conform to her crabbed ideas of what was right and proper.

Once, after a long absence, when I was about twenty-five, I returned to Eling on a golden September afternoon in time for a tea-party on the lawn. I put on a dress of old gold shantung which I fancied might please Aunt Margaret.

I was quickly disillusioned. As I chatted to one of the guests I heard Aunt Margaret remark loudly—so loudly that I knew that I was meant to overhear: 'Carrie dear, who is that gaudy figure in the yellow dress?'

'Hush, dear,' said Aunt Caroline in a low voice, 'that is Ida.'

Aunt Margaret let out a characteristic sigh. 'Oh dear! How unfortunate! So gaudy!'

I was still young enough to feel deeply wounded. Nor was that the end of it. At supper I found myself seated next to Aunt Margaret. With deceptive gentleness my Aunt began at once: 'My dear, did you notice how nice dear Violet and Gladys looked? So quiet, so ladylike.' Violet and Gladys, daughters of a neighbouring landowner, had worn, most inappropriately considering the glory of the day, dark grey coats and skirts and black felt hats.

I should have replied frankly that I thought they looked revoltingly dull, but the deeply ingrained habit of treating the Aunts with too much respect and never answering them back kept me silent.

Aunt Margaret loved, too, to belittle our activities. When I, engaged then in social work in London, said I must return for a meeting, Aunt Margaret with a malicious look in her small green eyes, remarked softly—and with a gentle sigh: 'My dear, you think yourself so important and busy, don't you? But I wonder what is the good of it all?'

Twice in talking of Aunt Margaret I have used the words 'if only'—if only this, if only that. But the biggest 'if only' may perhaps have been her rejection—or her parents' rejection—of her single proposal of marriage. When she was still young an expert arrived to clean the Gainsborough. Encouraged by her interest in his work and by her artistic talent he asked her to marry him. What her personal feeling for him may have been is unknown, but at all events she acquiesced in the decision that a girl in her position could not ally herself with a picture-cleaner.

Had she accepted his proposal the horrid metamorphosis that overtook her might have been averted. As it was, malice and a natural tendency to greed increased. Each week, in the solitude of her bedroom, she devoured a pound of clotted cream sent from Cornwall. Dante, Milton, Ruskin, stood untouched on her shelves. Venus rose unnoticed behind the tulip tree. 'The Wings of the Morning' grew dusty on its easel. Yet still she tried to keep alive an illusion that she moved in an ethereal world that few could enter.

Nevertheless, in the end I was able to recapture the image of the Aunt we loved in childhood—the Aunt who sat smiling at us sweetly from her divan, pouring out tea in elegant little cups to the silvery notes of a xylophone.

Aunt Louisa, as I have already said, was the Aunt who took definite charge of us, who worked the hardest to make us happy, yet was never a favourite with us.

This was partly due to the wide-open eye that she kept on

our activities and her numerous admonitions, which included among a hundred other things the washing of our hands, the wiping of our feet, and keeping off the wet lawns which, tree-studded and mossy, were, she maintained, probably with some justice, the wettest in the world.

It was also due to her habit of shooting brusque little questions at us about our doings at home, about my mother, about the books we read, about our friends, in fact about anything and everything. Perhaps we should not have minded this so much if my mother had not so repeatedly emphasized that Aunt Louisa was inquisitive that we came to think of curiosity as one of the deadly sins. Her possession of a large bump of it must be freely granted. You had only to look at her sharp little nose to recognize it: there can be no doubt that she enjoyed prying into other people's affairs too much. But her interest in ourselves was a different matter. We were the children that she had never borne, and every detail of our lives was of the utmost interest to her. Only long afterwards did we realize this, and the genuine affection that lay behind her curiosity. As it was, all too often we wished resentfully that she could paint an everlasting picture like Aunt Margaret, or hide herself away as securely as Aunt Selina at the end of a dark passage.

But she had one virtue in the eyes of my sisters and my-self: she really liked girls better than boys, and placed us on at least an equal footing with my elder brother. Victorian deference for the male was strong in all the other Aunts, but Aunt Louisa felt none of it, and the receptions in her room were especially for nieces.

It was a pleasant ordinary little room with no artistic pre-tensions. But the cupboards were stacked with treasures to delight the heart of a child. One was a doll's tea-set of charming design, another a zither, another some exotic shells that sailors had brought home from their voyages and sold in Southampton. My particular affection was for an odd-looking doll named Esmeralda guarded carefully since Aunt Louisa's own childhood. She must always be treated with extreme gentleness and only nursed in the safety of an armchair. Certainly she looked very frail with her long, thin, flexible kid body, her pale mournful face, her faded blue eyes. Her waxen cheeks were stained and marked in a way which suggested that tears had been shed over her. I think that she—and Aunt Caroline—had always shared Aunt Louisa's secret sorrows. Poor Aunt Louisa! I am sure that she, more than any other Aunt, had passionately longed to be married. And once, once only, had it appeared possible. A favourite cousin who often came to the house had singled her out for special favour—or so she and her sisters believed. So when, after a long absence, he wrote that he had a particular reason for wishing to see them all again, there was much significant nodding of heads among the sisters over the letter. On a beautiful afternoon in June the hour for the cousin's visit drew near and Aunt Caroline was seen accompanying Aunt Louisa to the hayfield adjoining the house. Here Aunt Caroline selected a large haycock, carefully seated her sister under it in a becoming attitude, and then retired.

The cousin duly arrived and was sent in search of Aunt Louisa, watched, I am sure, from behind upper windows, by four pairs of anxious eyes. But alas, he had only come to tell the family—and Aunt Louisa first of all—that he was engaged to be married.

Thus ended her only romance. She was too old by then to weep with Esmeralda, and Aunt Caroline's kind shoulders must have received her grief. To the cousin she never betrayed a hint of what she had suffered on his account, and later she became a devoted godmother to one of his daughters.

Among Aunt Louisa's most likable qualities was her zest for life. All the Aunts possessed it in some degree, but she more than any of the others. No sooner did we arrive at Eling than she began to plan outings and parties that gave her as much pleasure as they gave us. This power of enjoyment combined with her genuine interest in other people led to her possession of more friends than the rest. She used even sometimes to go abroad with companions chosen from outside the family circle, and was actually staying with two friends in Italy when she felt suddenly ill. An urgent wish to be at home seized her and she set out immediately. A few days later she died, surrounded by her sisters, with Aunt Carry's arm about her.

'God's little lamb!' breathed Aunt Margaret. I can imagine the tartness with which Aunt Louisa would have snapped back: 'Don't be ridiculous, Margie!'

Always so brisk and alert in her movements but with a far weaker constitution than her sisters, she had stolen a march on them in the matter of death and departed when she was only seventy-three, whereas they lived on into their nineties.

On our next visit to Eling, it seemed strange and a little flat not to be continually dodging Aunt Louisa, not to hear her thin imperative voice calling us out of the Wilderness, not to see her eager nose thrust forward round the corner of the verandah or at the foot of the back stairs, as she waited to waylay us.

And if the days brought more peace they also brought less sense of urgency now that her eager inquiring spirit had fled from the house.

Aunt Caroline was the true mother of the family, the wise, kind, solid figure who held the household together.

Without her restraining influence, her good judgment,

such antagonists as Aunt Selina, Aunt Margaret and Aunt Louisa could never have remained under one roof. As it was, a quiet word from her invariably cut short a squabble, and a single rebuke had almost instant effect.

Alone among the five she was no amateur. She was an expert housewife who, though she carried out no practical tasks herself, understood the ordering of good meals, the keeping of accounts, the making of butter, the choosing of meat, the feeding of the hens, the pigs, and the Alderney cow. She knew how a large garden should be stocked, a greenhouse heated, vines pruned. Through her tact she bound Matilda to the household for half a century. Elizabeth, a livelier, less contented creature, grew tired of the perpetual company of spinsters and fled after twenty years. The cook, and of course the young kitchen-maids, were never permanent. That cooks came and went was scarcely surprising, for their job was certainly no light one. Not only must they produce three hot meals a day, cakes and scones for tea and make butter twice a week, but also practise the most rigid economy under their mistress's watchful eye.

Another of Aunt Caroline's special activities was the keeping of close contact with a missionary who worked in Labrador among the Esquimaux. She wrote him long letters regularly and despatched constant parcels of every conceivable thing that might prove useful. In return he sent her lively accounts of his work and specimens of the things his people made, including a quilt of eider-down. He was her hero, and she spoke of him in a hushed, intense voice which she never used in speaking of anyone else. On one supreme occasion he came to stay, and from all that was said he must have been treated in a way that nobody, not even my father, had ever known. All five hovered round him anticipating his smallest wish. Though we never saw him, he remained a legend for us children and we were allowed to hear extracts from his letters, and to pass our fingers occasionally over the eider-down quilt under which Aunt Caroline slept each night.

She was also the principal dog-lover; but here her sound common-sense failed her. One after another, new dogs were introduced into the house and exercised religiously every day, but one after the other they died from pampering and over-feeding. There was Jock, the beautiful black-and-white Pomeranian of whom I have already spoken, so highly bred that he was a bag of nerves. During a children's party, when a little girl shook her croquet mallet at him because he tried to move her ball, he had a fit of hysterics that lasted several hours. Aunt Caroline and Aunt Mary took it in turns to sit beside him till he grew quiet again.

Then there was Nansen, an Esquimaux dog, presented by the missionary. With his dazzling white coat and jet-black eyes he was by far the handsomest and also the most masculine of all Aunt Caroline's acquisitions. But he too did not long survive the surfeit of food and affection.

Though dangerously soft-hearted where dogs were concerned, Aunt Caroline was perhaps a little over-severe with people, a little too uncompromising. Excessively honest herself, she could not bear the smallest deviation from the truth, and she would listen with a rigid face to my mother telling a lively story. The one had a gift for harmless embroidery, the other never uttered one word that was not strictly factual. Also, Aunt Caroline's sense of justice and her high standards of conduct for everyone (including herself) sometimes brought a rather arctic quality into the conversation.

We might, perhaps, start saying something which would have seemed all right at home, and then realize from our Aunt's face that it was all wrong at Eling. Our small attempt at a joke, our endeavour to amuse, would die an untimely death.

Thus, though we respected and admired her, the slight awe in which we held her prevented us from loving Aunt Caroline whole-heartedly until we were much older.

And yet she was immensely kind, continually ready to sacrifice herself both for us and for others, a prop to lean upon in time of trouble. If Aunt Margaret was a willow and Aunt Selina a box-bush, Aunt Caroline was an oak-tree. Any impression of hardness or asceticism that I may have given is false. Like all the Aunts she had a tremendous capacity for enjoyment. She loved horses and the countryside—though she could not rhapsodize about it like Aunt Margaret. She loved picnics and treats and travelling. She was by far the best-looking of the sisters, and if she never married it may possibly have been because ordinary young men felt slightly rebuffed by her manner.

There was one person towards whom Aunt Caroline could never show severity; one person who could do no wrong in her sight; one person on whom she lavished all the tenderness and love of which she was capable: and that was Aunt Mary.

These two younger sisters were bound together by the deepest ties of affection, and if they could have shared a small home together—just the two of them—they would have been completely happy. But, as it was, their constant mediation was essential to keep the eternal bickering of the other three in check. Aunt Mary, though she stayed in the background as much as possible, was always at hand to help Aunt Caroline in her role of peacemaker. Less severe and authoritative, more pliant, she deferred to Aunt Caroline in everything.

It was Aunt Mary who worked hardest to counteract the

evil influences at work beyond the Toll Gate. Not only did she visit the old and sick in the village and take them the time-honoured offerings of soup, calves-foot jelly and custard, but she valiantly met the enemy on his own ground and held a Bible class for young men in a corrugated-iron room in the heart of the red-brick abomination. What influence she wielded I shall never know, but certainly it was a heroic effort.

Often she returned home exhausted and dispirited, or with a raging headache, conscious that she had been beating in vain against a closed door. For she had no training that could help her to deal with the difficulties of unbelievers.

Aunt Caroline was always at hand to welcome her back and provide her with a cup of tea. 'Dearest Mary, how was it tonight?' she would ask.

'Hard, very hard. That Sam Thorn plagues me with such questions and there is so much sniggering.'

Aunt Caroline would rest her arm for a moment about Mary's waist and turn a look of deep sympathy upon her.

Aunt Mary's outlook on contemporary life was wider than that of her sisters. When the prolonged miners' strike raged in the early part of the century, she never joined in the general denunciations characteristic of her class but ranged herself beside Lord Lansdowne in his call for a more generous understanding of the men's hardships.

Of all the Aunts she undoubtedly tried hardest to apply her religion to daily life. Her reading was less confined, more modern. We suspected that sometimes she read novels of which the older sisters, at all events, would have disapproved. Once looking from our window in the early morning we saw her sitting absorbed in a book under the oak-tree. Suddenly some sound from the house, the closing of a door or the opening of a window, seemed to warn her of possible disturbance. She closed the book hastily and glided away among the trees.

Whereas Aunt Margaret as she grew old resembled a tree whose fruit gradually turns rotten, Aunt Mary was like one that blossoms more freely with age, whose scent grows steadily sweeter. Her more tiresome characteristics—her tendency to archness, to trade on being the baby of the family, her occasional malice towards my mother, who made much fun of her behind her back—gradually fell away from her, and she became ever more likable, more valiant in her struggle to do what she believed to be right.

III

The Daily Round

More than for any people I have ever known the Daily Round appeared to provide the Aunts with all that they needed. If at some time in their lives there had been vague discontents, hankerings after a different kind of existence, unspoken (most certainly unspoken) regrets for their unmarried state, by the time I knew them these no longer troubled them. Day after day, year after year, a smooth current, as gentle as the tide in Southampton Water, carried them forward. Sometimes it might be ruffled by apprehension at that horrid growth beyond the Toll Gate; sometimes by a cook giving notice or being dismissed; sometimes by the hostility between them and my mother reaching a climax; more often by squabbles between the three elder Aunts. But that was all.

No doubts, no uneasy questioning as to the nature and purpose of the universe, ever troubled them. An agnostic was a diseased person who only needed a proper course of treatment to be restored to spiritual health, and they did what they could for the few—the very few—who came their way, by carefully chosen tracts.

Nor did they question the rightness of the social order. Poverty and charity must go hand-in-hand for ever.

Politically they stood on equally firm ground. The Con-

servative Party represented sound government, justice for
all, the upholding of the moral law, the maintenance of a way
of life equally right for themselves, for their men-servants
and their maid-servants, for the cottagers beyond their gates.
It stood four-square against the army of dissenters, free-
thinkers, self-seekers, demagogues.

Let the Radicals in and the flood would sweep down the
Toll Gate, bringing ruin and evil in its wake.

This apprehension continually goaded them to fresh
efforts on behalf of the Primrose League—even to tiresome
attendances at evening meetings somewhere beyond the
Toll Gate—but it could not, in earlier years at all events,
disturb the even tenor of their lives. God and the Conserva-
tives must triumph in the end. Lloyd George was still an
obscure little Welsh whipper-snapper and his potentiality for
evil not yet a nightmare.

So each day, fortified by early morning tea, serene, un-
troubled, they answered the summons of the big gong in the
hall to breakfast and family prayers.

At one end of the long dining-room knelt the maids in
their starched print dresses and caps: Matilda, Elizabeth,
the cook and the kitchen-maid; at the other end, the Aunts
and ourselves. The cage of Sobo, the grey parrot, was
shrouded in a black cloth to ensure his silence, though occasionally he broke into horrid shrieks and had to be carried
from the room. Once, when the black shroud was removed
at the end of prayers, an extraordinary thing had happened.
Sobo, quite an old bird and previously believed to be a male,
had laid an egg in the bottom of her cage.

It was Elizabeth who discovered it.

'Come and look here, miss!' she cried to Aunt Caroline.

Aunt Caroline looked, and beckoned to Aunt Mary. Soon
all the Aunts were clustered round the cage staring at this

phenomenon. Sobo herself sat with her head on one side, enjoying her notoriety.

But to return to family prayers. The Aunt whose turn it was to read on that particular morning knelt at the head of the table with a large prayer-book, and waited till the doors were shut to begin. But when the first prayer was half over, or when we were well into the second or third, there would come the sounds of subdued scurrying in the hall and of the door being opened furtively. Then Aunt Margaret, breathless and a little unbuttoned, dropped on her knees beside the nearest chair. If Aunt Caroline or Aunt Mary were reading they ignored her. But if it were Aunt Selina or Aunt Louisa they turned a dark look in her direction, and paused till her last sigh, her last flutter, was over.

A different Aunt read prayers each day, and each one made them sound entirely different. Only the pronunciation of God as 'Gord' and Ah-men as 'A-men' remained the same. Aunt Margaret usually lost her turn. I seem to remember her arriving in time only once. On this occasion Aunt Louisa already had possession of the prayer-book when Aunt Margaret, unusually dishevelled, glided in, took the book firmly from her and also her place at the head of the table. In melting tones, barely above a whisper, she besought God to have mercy on us.

The breakfast that followed prayers was an ample one. Porridge (cereals were unknown at that time) was followed by a hot dish: eggs and bacon or kidneys on toast, or kippers; and there was often a ham on the sideboard as well. Toast, orange and quince marmalade, a large pat of deep yellow butter, salt, pepper, sugar, all stood on a dumb-waiter in the middle of the table. It was our delight to spin it round as fast as we dared, but after one of us had shot everything off and made a shocking mess we were forced to treat it more cautiously. Letters, which seemed largely to consist of charitable appeals (each Aunt subscribed to her own special causes and was not easily wooed by new competitors), were usually laid aside till the important business of eating was over.

Aunt Louisa ate least and kept a sharp eye on our plates. For some reason, we never quite understood why, it was wrong to make your toast exactly match your butter and marmalade. I suppose she thought we might spread them on too thickly at the end.

Breakfast over, the Aunts slipped away one by one to their common tasks. What those common tasks were we never discovered, but all five sisters managed to give the impression that they were immensely busy. I am still puzzled as to how they spent their mornings. For I never remember seeing one of them with a duster, or making a bed except with Elizabeth's help, or washing up even a teacup, except once on a Sunday afternoon when on some special occasion all the maids were out together. Aunt Mary, looking very solemn and preoccupied, then requested me to dry for her while she washed. This she did with great deliberation and thoroughness, in complete silence except when she warned me at intervals to be very careful. It was evidently too anxious and exacting a business for conversation.

Aunt Caroline's activities were the most clearly defined. She would disappear into the kitchen for long consultations with the cook, after which followed interviews with White and Lever.

We could make a good guess as to how Aunt Margaret was occupying herself. Most probably, after a long period in her room, she had repaired to her studio.

But Aunt Selina's movements in her own fastness remained a complete mystery. Only when she fell off a chair, which happened from time to time, did we know that she had been tidying out one of her cupboards.

Aunt Mary was a little more visible. She alternated between the big room where she and Aunt Caroline slept together, and the little room where she dressed and undressed and wrote numerous letters. Also, we often saw her hurry out on some charitable errand in the village or on business connected with the school or the Bible Reading Society.

Aunt Louisa, of course, was never invisible. She was here, there and everywhere, poking her sharp little nose into all our activities, herding us up the back stairs when we started up the front ones, guarding the front steps, hunting for us when we had hidden in the Wilderness or among the rhododendrons.

Punctually at one o'clock the Aunts reassembled in the dining-room—for dinner if only we children were staying in the house, but if our parents were there too then late dinner was the order of the day. In either case it was always a substantial meal.

One by one the Aunts bustled in, murmuring how busy they had been. To hear them talking it always seemed that the morning was never long enough to accomplish all they had meant to do. Often Aunt Margaret conveyed the impression that she had hardly been able to tear herself from her painting, but certainly she never missed her food because of it.

Immediately after the midday meal a tea-tray was brought to the Blue Room or the verandah. The Aunts had a passion for tea—very pale, weak tea; they drank it at least five times a day. My mother, who didn't like a lot of tea but liked it strong, thought this a most pernicious habit and held it responsible for the internal rumblings in which the Aunts

excelled. Afterwards Aunt Margaret would go to her room
to rest. Aunt Selina would bury herself behind *The Times*,
Aunt Caroline and Aunt Mary would sit close to each other
discussing in low tones their past and future activities, while
Aunt Louisa hovered round with one eye on us and another
on them. For she was jealous of the deep affection between
the two youngest sisters. She adored Aunt Caroline, longed
to be first with her, but knew herself doomed always to fill
a secondary place.

Later there were visits to be paid in the village by one or
more Aunts. Aunt Mary must make a final effort to talk with
the vicar (a most elusive person, it appeared) about the behaviour of a choir-boy or the sad condition of the hassocks.
Aunt Caroline must take her dog for a walk. Or there were
calls to pay in the victoria. This was a most serious and important business, for the Aunts called regularly once a month
on all the more chosen of their friends. Newcomers were only
visited after searching inquiries into their character and
social status. Wealth alone carried no weight. At one time
anyone connected with business was taboo, but later this ban
was lifted in favour of those who attended church.

Fairly frequently there was a shopping expedition to
Southampton in the afternoon, or we might be invited to a
party or assist with one at Eling Manor. The Aunts spared
no pains to make these an outstanding success.

In the morning we helped Aunt Louisa and Aunt Mary
to carry out games from the Round House. But it was to
White that the setting-up of the croquet hoops fell because
he alone could be trusted to see that they were in a straight
line.

However, we were allowed to deal with the rainbow-
coloured balls, the stumps for rounders, and the bat, trap and
ball apparatus. Meanwhile the maids had laid a big carpet on

the lawn and set chairs all round it, and the cook busied herself with a multitude of small iced cakes decorated with silver balls and cherries and angelica.

By lunch-time most arrangements were complete, and we all went off to rest before the party began. But when the first guests arrived four Aunts, all smiles and kindness and graciousness, even Aunt Selina, were ready to receive them. Aunt Margaret, of course, was always a little late on the scene, but the elegance of the floating white veil behind her hat and the jewels she had put on more than made up for it.

We could sympathize with Aunt Margaret because when we gave parties at home nobody was ever quite ready, and things had to be done at breakneck speed at the last moment. Once my mother, intensely proud of her new ice-making machine, hurriedly poured in the contents of a bottle of liquid soup-herbs instead of vanilla. When the ices were handed round strange expressions appeared on the faces of our guests. And sometimes it seemed as if my father's bees disliked parties and showed it in regrettable fashion. I shall never forget a parson with a bald head kneeling before my mother and crying: 'Who will rid me of this turbulent beast?' while a bee, entangled in his few hairs, buzzed ominously. At the Aunts' such catastrophes would have been impossible.

Always everything ran smoothly till the last victoria, the last dog-cart, the last modest pony-trap, had driven away. No child had been allowed to feel bored or at a loss for a single moment.

But the Aunts were very tired when supper-time came.

If there were no parties or other engagements, then we often walked or rode in the Manor Woods, or went for a picnic.

The Manor Woods lay less than half a mile away and

seemed so much a part of the Aunts' domain that we used to believe they belonged to them, the more so as we never met anyone else there. Later we found that a wealthy neighbour was the owner and gave the Aunts special permission to walk in them.

We adored those woods. At home we were encircled on three sides by wide, almost treeless downs. We knew each hill-top, each grooved valley, each tuft of beeches, for miles round. They were our special kingdom to which we would return with undiminished affection. But meanwhile these woods of the Aunts cast a spell on us—and one that, in my own case at least, has never been broken. The mere mention of them brings back the warm, moist, scented air that met you the moment you passed through the white gates; the stillness; the sense that there was a world imperfectly explored and always rich in secrets and surprises.

Even the Aunts appeared transformed when they walked in the Manor Woods. But not Aunt Selina. Enclosed for ever in the walls that she had built up round herself, she appeared unchanged and unchangeable—except on that one occasion when she taught us 'Lubey Loo'. Yet it may well be that we were mistaken in this, and that she drew a quiet satisfaction from the scene that neither her face nor her tongue could express.

As for Aunt Margaret, in the Woods she became a kind of aeolian harp. As she leant her long lean body against the trunk of a tree, rapturous sighs and faint exclamations were drawn from her by the scent of the honeysuckle, the light on the tree-tops, the song of a bird. Such a response seemed natural in her. She never moved far, for she was a poor walker, and we left her to her private ecstasies. From the other three we did not expect ecstasy. But it beat its way out all the same, even if less vocally. In the Manor Woods, a long tradition of nature-worship, inherited perhaps from their Cornish ancestors, came to life in the Aunts. Their faces changed and softened. Talk about the Primrose League, of Aunt Mary's Bible class, of the misdoings of politicians, ceased. The danger on the other side of the Toll Gate was forgotten. They were at peace.

For us, nearly everything in the Manor Woods was rare and strange. We knew and loved the flowers of the chalk: milkwort, eyebright, rock-roses and all those others that made our downs a sea of colour in summer. But here were flowers of more luxuriant character such as we never saw at home. There were foxgloves, most magical of flowers; rose-pink musk-mallow instead of our humble common one; bugles taller and more triumphantly blue than in our ditches; clusters of starry centaury; and yellow water-lilies that made us catch our breath when we came on them suddenly in a little lake among the trees.

The birds and butterflies, too, seemed to us almost tropical: the jays, the woodpeckers, the nuthatches swinging their bodies against the tree trunks, the silver-washed fritillaries and Painted Ladies, and once a Purple Emperor soaring high among the oaks. But more malevolent insects sometimes invaded the Woods.

Once Aunt Mary and I fled before a swarm of huge mosquitoes which, she declared, arrived on ships docked at Southampton. It was the only time I remember our peace being disturbed. Clutching me with one hand and beating the air with the other, she ran till she was red and breathless, and when she reached home had to lie on a sofa with a bottle of smelling-salts.

No account of the Manor Woods can be complete without Tommy. His stout white body, his kindly nature, is indissolubly bound up with them. He carried us each in turn along the grass paths at an easy trot. The ground, unlike the firm surface of our downs, was too soft and boggy for anything else; moreover, he was probably too old to canter. It was not only us children whom he carried. Sometimes an Aunt mounted him.

I remember Aunt Louisa, wearing a close-fitting dress of blue and white foulard, and on her head a wide shady hat draped with white tulle, being carried along, sedate and very upright, in front of us. The sight of her struck me as irresistibly comic.

'How funny Aunt Louisa looks!' I cried to Aunt Caroline. I must have been very young indeed to venture such a remark. Aunt Caroline, always a staunch defender of Aunt Louisa, stopped and fixed her eyes severely on me.

'Aunt Louisa doesn't look funny at all. She looks beautiful,' she said. 'You may be thankful if you can ever sit a horse as straight as she.'

Her expression and her tone taught me a lesson I never forgot. No Aunt, least of all Aunt Louisa, must ever again be spoken of as funny.

Picnics at the Aunts' were very grand.

My mother used to plan delightful and unusual picnics high on top of the downs; or picnics were carried for miles in rowing boats along our quiet canal; or to satisfy the hunger of a skating party, the gardener trundled on a wheelbarrow a hamper of hot mince-pies and a can of soup, wrapped in blankets to keep it warm.

The Aunts' picnics were quite different; we drove in the waggonette with Lever in attendance, wearing his green coat, his white leggings, his top hat. If the chosen place was the heath, high above the Manor Woods, then there was a silver urn heated by a spirit-lamp, because a fire would be dangerous. Aunt Carry and Aunt Mary would sit down with pre-

occupied faces to set out tea on a large white cloth, while Aunt Louisa, happy, but I am afraid often frustrated by our behaviour, pursued us as we threw ourselves about madly in the heather, or searched for sundew and asphodels in the bogs; until she, a little flushed, and we, golden with pollen, eventually sat down to a delicious meal. A few yards away Hazel and Walnut champed and chafed, and Lever, bare-headed and unbuttoned, drank his tea beside them.

At picnics in the New Forest (only a few miles away) we generally made a fire—or rather, Lever did—to which we contributed a few sticks. That done, we raced along the smooth paths that ran like little rivers through the under-growth, trying to evade Aunt Louisa by hiding behind the trees, or pressing ourselves into hollow stumps. For me, with my passion for fairy tales, the Forest was an ideal back-ground for lost children, hunting princes, old women poking wrinkled, wicked faces out of the shadows. But I never spoke of such things to the Aunts. They liked sensible stories with a good moral. Sometimes, in the earliest days that I remem-ber, instead of a picnic we had tea with my father's only brother, George, who lived in a white house on the edge of the Forest with his wife, Dora. Of her, my most abiding recollection is her voice, rich and deep, as she came out to welcome us.

Uncle George could not join her because of the terrible fall from a tree he had had as a boy, which now condemned him to lie on a couch or be pushed in a wheeled chair. Yet when we met him at the tea-table he seemed cheerful enough, with his rather red face and loud voice. Once, we were told, he had been a gay and dashing young man who, the first effects of his accident over, had for a time driven about the countryside in a high dog-cart and had also hunted. Some-how in spite of the solicitous way in which they hung about his chair, he didn't seem quite to belong to the Aunts nor they to him.

To me Uncle George was inextricably bound up with William Rufus, because the stone marking the spot where the king fell with an arrow in his heart was close to my uncle's house.

Another picnicking place beloved of the Aunts was Crackner Hard, in those days ramshackle, unfrequented, delightful, where one or two builders of small boats had their wooden sheds and where the pleasant sound of hammering rang out above the ripple of the tide. Here tea was a much less ceremonious meal—perhaps to suit the character of the place or because the carriage and horses were left at the end of the lane. At any rate all the food was produced from string bags.

Opposite us Southampton could be seen and the hum and throb of its life floated across the water. The Aunts took intense interest in the movements of all the big ships, and sat on the beach peering through their opera-glasses at them, and murmuring their lordly names.

Now industrialism has broken through their Toll Gate, stalked grimly across their kingdom, pounced on every small secret corner, and I can imagine only too well the expression on their faces if they were to come driving down to Crackner Hard today.

But dearly as they loved these quiet retreats beside the Water, they loved Southampton too and felt an almost personal pride in its importance, its size, its fame. As long as all those magnificent ships came and went Britannia's claim to rule the waves would remain undisputed. When we stayed at Eling we knew we should pay at least two visits to the city.

Sometimes the grey horses took us there, and on these occasions packing into the waggonette became an even more

complicated business than usual because of all the shopping
bags and the parcels of goods, sent on approval, to be returned. Matilda and Elizabeth scurried in and out of the
house with these, and with holland rugs to lay over our knees
and long dust-cloaks of tussore silk to be draped round the
Aunts' shoulders. They also helped the older sisters to climb
to their seats, and made sure that each had her parasol or
umbrella, whichever seemed the more appropriate. All this
never took less than twenty minutes, more if Aunt Margaret
was of the party.

How different was this departure from a journey to
Devizes, our own little market-town, with our grubby
gardener bringing round old Rose and the Ark, and the
family running across the hall and leaping in one by one, till
at the end of the drive the last panting child scrambled up
behind.

Equipped for all emergencies, off we set at last, packed
tightly in a double row. Aunt Caroline always sat beside
Lever on the box seat because she loved to watch the horses.
Through the Toll Gate—and if the miller kept them waiting
the Aunts' frigid manner showed their displeasure—through
the ugly red-brick town and along the dusty yellow road
beside the Water, we moved at a brisk pace till finally we
entered the city by a quiet back way, passed under an ancient
archway and burst suddenly into streets that, though free as
yet from motors, seemed to us teeming with traffic. When
we drew up outside the livery stables, our disembarking was
almost as complicated as our setting-off had been.

There were urgent decisions to be made about parasols or
umbrellas and overcoats, and an anxious scanning of the sky.
There were dust-cloaks to be discarded, bags to be fished out
from under the seats. Lever, holding the horses' heads,
looked on tolerantly, but sometimes with a hint of mischief

on his bland, handsome face. When in later years Beech
succeeded him the look tended to be sardonic.

From time to time, however, it was decided that we would
take the train from Redbridge, and this brought even greater
complications. For not only must the ascent into, and the
descent from, the waggonette be repeated, but there was
also the business of buying tickets and boarding the train. I
never remember a journey when it was not touch-and-go
whether we caught the train or not. Each Aunt liked to take
her own ticket and to pay for one of us, and this involved the
hitching-up of skirts and a desperate search for the little
bags, suspended between petticoats, that were considered the
only safe means of carrying money. If Aunt Margaret was
among us the suspense was frightful. There stood the station-
master waiting to blow his whistle; there was the train panting to be gone; there were amused and curious passengers
watching from the windows; and there was Aunt Margaret
struggling frantically with an elusive purse, and revealing
glimpses of not less than three petticoats.

But I should be giving a false impression if I suggest that
we ourselves saw anything humorous in the scene. We felt
far too deeply involved, too ridden with anxiety, too em-
barrassed.

However, once we were all safely seated in our second-
class carriage, happiness took possession of us.

Southampton was by far the grandest town we knew, and
it offered a wide choice of attractions.

Perhaps we broke up into little parties for shopping and
met for tea at a shop near the Bargate. Or perhaps an Aunt
or two took us down to the docks, and even once arranged
for us to walk along the decks of an immense ship bound for
India. Or it may be that we went on the pier for a concert in
the glass-walled pavilion.

My pleasure on one such occasion was considerably spoilt at the outset by one of the Aunts' strange little economies. Generous in big things they would take absurd pains to save a few pence. So when it appeared that if two children were small enough to pass at once through one compartment of the turnstile they were admitted at half price, I and my brother were jammed together, and only extricated with difficulty. Our childish dignity was hurt, and we both felt very cross. However, good temper was restored by the time we had entered the pavilion and taken our seats in front of a magnificent military band. But what delighted me even more was an elegant lady in a Grecian robe who played a golden harp. I sat beside Aunt Margaret and for once it was I who quivered responsively. She listened with an air of displeasure, and finally pronounced the Grecian lady to be vulgar and her playing poor.

A supreme event, and one not to be counted as part of the Daily Round, was the occasion on which we drove into Southampton for the Diamond Jubilee Naval Review. Again the picnic came from string bags—on the boat that took us out beyond the harbour—but my goodness, what did that matter compared with the glory that shone out as darkness fell and all the ships suddenly appeared decked in thousands of flashing, many-coloured lights!

It hardly seemed possible there was so much beauty in the world. The Aunts were full of suppressed pride and excitement, but poor Aunt Margaret developed one of her special headaches and had to go down to the cabin.

On really hot afternoons, when outings would have been too exhausting for the Aunts, deck-chairs were placed under the trees and leisurely games of croquet played.

On wet days they busied themselves with crochet and embroidery. Never do I remember an Aunt doing anything so utilitarian as mending a stocking. Matilda and Elizabeth must have attended to that.

Meanwhile we romped in the verandah or fought at battle-dore and shuttlecock, or built houses on a little much-loved landing halfway up the back stairs, a place with a magic of its own that belonged to neither upstairs nor downstairs.

But whatever the order of the day, time never seemed to hang heavy on the Aunts' hands or on our own. Some important activity presented itself at every hour.

Often after tea, or supper, or 'High Tea', according to our age and the time of year, Aunt Louisa would bring out games from her cupboard in the Blue Room. Foremost among these was the beautiful polished cream halma box, with all the little red, white, green and black men packed in their separate compartments. Soon they were all struggling to cross the board in a wild multi-coloured maze, hopping deliciously over each other, hurrying into safety before others seized their places. Never was Aunt Louisa more alert, more full of zest, than when she grasped one of her men in bony fingers and carried him on a long series of hops from one end of the board to the other. Her eyes glittered with excitement and she would let loose a small shrill burst of laughter. Another favourite game of hers was Reversi, played to the accompaniment of joyful shouts from someone who found the opportunity to change a whole row of counters to their own colour, or of deep groans when the process was reversed. Fox-and-Geese was more solemn and frightening. I still remember my helpless misery as Aunt Louisa's red fox pounced relentlessly this way and that, devouring my poor little ivory geese.

We all changed for the evening meal. If it was only High Tea then the Aunts wore dresses that had once served grander occasions, filled in at the neck with tulle if originally cut low: dresses of black lace over lilac or purple or white satin, dresses with an ample sweep at the back, and little frills at the throat and wrists. If our parents were staying in the house, or other important visitors, then there was full evening dress, a four-course dinner, and a bottle of wine. Strange to say this was usually bought from the local wine merchant in spite of rich stores laid down by my grandfather.

Only when my father was with them did Aunt Caroline accompany him to the cellar to choose a bottle of whatever met his fancy. When the last Aunt died the amount of port, claret and burgundy that, thick with mildew, had gradually perished, was unbelievable and heart-breaking.

We children watched Matilda and Elizabeth setting the table with silver and glass, and listened to the swish of an Aunt's long skirts as she hurried along the hall and took a peep in to see that all was as it should be. But such grandeur was not for us. A simpler supper awaited us in the Servants' Hall.

The evening meal over, and ourselves grown too old to be hurried straight to bed, we all repaired to the Blue Room, except on Sundays and special occasions when we sat in the big drawing-room. The Blue Room was so much a part of the Aunts that one felt neither could have existed without the other. The walls were covered with a sky-blue and white satin-like paper, the sofa and chairs were upholstered in brocade to match. I don't believe there was one really comfortable chair, according to our modern standards; which was perhaps why all the Aunts, except Aunt Margaret, had such straight backs. Each had her own special seat where no one else dreamed of sitting. A placid picture of cows by Paul Potter or more adventurous pictures of ships at sea by Van de Veldt hung on the walls.

Again tea was brought in and, when each Aunt had drunk

at least two cups, what my mother called the 'Evening Concert' began.

Strange rumblings and gurglings issued now from one corner of the room, now from another. It was difficult to decide which Aunt was enriching the orchestra at any given moment. But we learned to place the sounds by the little movements, the gentle shufflings, the clearing of the throat, with which they attempted to disguise or drown their contributions. Gradually the full volume died away and only a few faint echoes broke out now and again.

Each Aunt, seated in a chair facing the large lamp on the round mahogany table, busied herself with a book or a piece of needlework. We had been taught to sit with our backs to the light, but not so the Aunts. They faced it uncompromisingly. If darkness had not yet fallen an interval always elapsed between the time when reading grew impossible and Matilda's entry to light the lamp and draw the shutters. For this the Aunts' propensity for small economies was partly responsible, but they also, especially Aunt Margaret, thought it restful and beautiful to sit in the twilight. We ourselves, deep in our story books, found it excessively boring. When the weather was very chilly there might be a fire, but I seldom remember one. Generally we stayed at Eling during the six months when none was thought necessary. Summer fires were undreamed-of no matter how cold it might be, and in fact the small room, with shutters bolted and curtains drawn, often seemed uncomfortably warm.

As we grew older and our ideas on fresh air stronger we would sometimes seize a moment when some Aunts were half asleep or buried in their books, to unfasten a shutter surreptitiously and slip out through the french window. If we could plead the nightingale singing in the oak-tree close to the house, that caused Aunt Margaret to fall into raptures

—then all was well. But we soon realized that here great caution must be shown. Once we produced him in a wrong month, and our explanation for leaving the room was coldly received.

On one particular evening I remember vividly how the atmosphere of the Blue Room suddenly seemed oppressive with old age. It hung in the air like a heavy fog. It closed in round me and weighed me down.

Aunt Selina's head was nodding spasmodically and her parted lips were moist. Aunt Margaret's head had fallen sideways and her cap drooped over one eye. Aunt Louisa, upright as ever, sat with closed eyes. Aunt Caroline's face was drawn and tired as the light fell full on it, and her embroidery had slipped from her fingers. Aunt Mary, her book held close to her short-sighted eyes, continued to read.

I could bear it no longer. I exchanged a hasty glance with a younger sister, and we made a furtive exit into the garden. It was a windy autumn night and the air was filled with the

S.W.A. 65

sound of dead leaves. Away we ran along the path that encircled the garden till the house was left as far behind as possible. Only a crack of light from the open shutter gleamed through the darkness. I seemed to see again the five Aunts sitting there, faded and old and tired, their powers slipping from them, waiting for Death (who, however, did not fetch away four of them till long, long after that). In fierce revulsion I faced the wind and drew deep breaths, while my heart cried: 'Oh, God, don't let me grow old. Never, never let me grow old!' I must have been thirteen then.

But the inescapable scent of autumn and the mocking tinkle of dead leaves filled the air. The voice of a brown owl quavered across the lawn. My sister, too young to share my passionate revolt, was capering wildly along the path. When eventually we returned soberly to the Blue Room, the Aunts were engaged in the evening bustle that always preceded bedtime—plumping out the cushions, straightening the chairs, tidying the books, getting ready for evening prayers.

Aunt Louisa's sharp eyes fastened on us.

'My dears, what have you been doing out in the dark?' she asked.

'Listening to an owl,' I answered.

She nodded kindly. 'Come with me and you shall have some hot lemonade. You look cold.'

'Such foolishness! It's their own fault,' grumbled Aunt Selina.

As I sipped the sweet hot drink my moment of rebellion passed. Somehow perhaps I would manage to circumvent old age, and after all it was natural to be tired at night. Tomorrow morning the Aunts would seem ageless again, borne on a stream of energy that never failed, renewing their plans for the Daily Round. Nor, to do them justice, did they ever appear to mind growing old; if they did they never spoke of it. And that, after all, is the right and gallant way to behave, especially in the company of the young.

The secret must be kept—the sad, dark secret.

The golden-voiced clock on the chimney-piece struck ten, and this was echoed on a more sombre note from the dining-room by a marble and bronze clock known to us as Old Father Time, because of the figure on the top. We all knelt down, each beside our own chair. 'Lighten our darkness,' prayed the Aunt appointed for the evening.

Then we moved into the long dim hall where a row of silver candlesticks stood waiting to take us all to bed.

IV

Sunday at the Aunts'

Sunday at home was one thing; at Eling quite another. To begin with, apart from a ban on tennis and croquet, we could play such games and read such books as we pleased in our Wiltshire vicarage. But there was quite a storm when we took Ludo from the Blue Room cupboard and were caught in the very act of throwing the dice. At home we read what we pleased, but the Aunts only allowed stories with a high moral purpose. *The Fairchild Family* was a particular favourite of theirs and this posed us with an awkward problem. For my mother always treated it as a humorous work and read it aloud with the sole object of extracting as much amusement as possible from its more ludicrous passages. But the Aunts took it in perfect seriousness.

Once, in my early 'teens, I grabbed a volume of Molière from the bookshelf. Sitting on the sunny verandah I felt extremely self-satisfied, sustained by a belief that to read French was meritorious at any time. Suddenly Aunt Selina stood squinting down at me suspiciously.

'My dear, what have you there?' she asked.

I told her with pride, confident that even she, dry-hearted old thing though she was, would be bound to express approval.

Her reaction startled me.

'Molière!' she cried in horror. 'I don't consider Molière

at all fit reading for Sunday! Put your book back on the shelf
at once.' Her face twitched violently. Her mouth worked.

And then there was the question of attendance at church.

At home, after struggling into shoes and stockings, and
hastily putting on hats, we answered—at the last possible
moment—the call of the bells, burst into the garden, jumped
the ha-ha and ran across the field, pursued sometimes by our
wicked pony (who once assaulted even my father and bit a
hole in the sleeve of his cassock) or by a certain ferocious
cockerel, or by an over-affectionate drake who had a passion
for following me into church.

Even if the service often seemed a little tedious (since my
father spared his congregation neither the ante-communion
service nor the Litany), at all events we felt completely at
home. There were the Kings and Bishops looking down on
us from the lofty roof, and below them all the familiar
village faces and figures—old Squire Ruddle with his side-
whiskers and shabby broadcloth coat in front of us, pretending to kneel when the right time came; his horsy nephew;
his cousin Lizzie Giddings in her ancient grey cloak, with a
stocking round her throat if the weather was cold; the row
of well-groomed, good-looking sons from the farm under
Easton Hill. There was Tom Merritt, the tenor, whose great
voice must, we thought, reverberate even into the spire; Mr
Moss, the sexton, tidying up each prayer with an immense
Amen—and all the rest of them. Packed together in our pew
we could exchange secretive smiles when my father said
something in his sermon that struck us as funny. Once it
seemed so excruciatingly comic that we broke into irre-
pressible giggles. In vain we buried our faces in our handkerchiefs, my father's eyes were on us, and he paused till we
could behave ourselves again.

But at Eling church-going was a different and far intenser

affair. Even to smile was reprehensible; to giggle would have been blasphemy.

One of the Aunts' favourite texts was: 'Behold how joyful and pleasant a thing it is to serve the Lord'; and another: 'I was glad when they said unto me, Come, let us go up to the house of the Lord.' But we were not glad at all when Aunt Louisa called us from the verandah to get ready for morning service.

To have driven in state behind Hazel and Walnut would have offered some compensation, but on no pretext whatever were the horses ever taken out on a Sunday. So there was nothing for it but to prepare for the ceremonious communal departure that differed so widely from our own piecemeal exit.

Though the Aunts really could have had nothing to do since breakfast (except possibly make their own beds to save the maids), there was always a frantic bustle at the last moment. Only Aunt Louisa was invariably punctual so that she might see that our stockings were properly pulled up and our hats well down on our foreheads.

Aunt Selina had forgotten her purse, Aunt Mary had dropped a glove, or someone's golosh had hidden itself in a dark corner of the passage. Perhaps Sunday was more often wet than other days; perhaps goloshes were an essential part of church uniform—worn to make sure that you arrived not only dry-shod but also with no dirt on your shoes. At all events I never remember an occasion when five pairs were not brought out and when five Aunts were not sitting about on stools and benches, tugging that revolting flabbiness over their shoes. Aunt Margaret, of course, was never ready and Aunt Carry, in command, would send one of the maids as usual to hurry her down from her room. Nobody would have dreamed of leaving her to make her way alone. Just as the sisters stuck together in home life, so they would stick together during the walk to church.

Pale, breathless, her hair slightly dishevelled under her bonnet, Aunt Margaret, as likely as not, with one golosh only half on, came down the steps at the last possible moment.

I mention her bonnet. Bonnets, in our earlier days, were considered by the Aunts an absolute necessity for a properly dressed woman on a Sunday, and it was part of their grievance against my mother that she refused to wear one. When she stayed at Eling she provided some light relief to the scene because of the funny contrast that she presented in her smart, tight, Redfern suit, her jaunty hat, her small, high-heeled shoes. All the Aunts, except Aunt Selina, had very large, very flat feet which of course looked all the larger in goloshes.

So, at last, there we all were, moving in a straggling procession along the sandy road, while the maids, also in bonnets, followed at a respectful distance; and I am sure that nobody, looking at the Aunts, could have detected any signs of gladness. There was only anxiety in the air—anxiety lest they should be late, anxiety lest the hems of their long black skirts and moiré petticoats should be soiled. It was on Sundays that we really saw the shape of the Aunts' legs as they looped their dresses high over their arms. And if they still had any anxiety to spare it was turned on us. Perhaps one of our hated stockings was ruckled about the ankle, or our hats tipped back too far from our foreheads—a most vulgar habit. Aunt Louisa's alert eyes never failed to notice such defects.

Moving faster than any Aunt really liked, we usually managed to enter the church porch as the last bell was sounding, while Aunt Margaret was still toiling up the steep path at the end.

And now there was a pause while goloshes were discarded

71

at varying speeds. Aunt Mary could kick hers off quickly, but the others, seated on the stone bench, found it a more painful operation. The urgency of getting into our pew before the service actually began caused a break-up in our ranks.

Aunt Margaret was abandoned, and we hurried in as fast as golosh-disposal permitted.

Aunt Louisa pushed us into our right places, each of us between two Aunts. Aunt Caroline dispensed prayer and hymn books from a large red box with a padded lid, that also served as a hassock. And now at last it seemed to me that they could say their favourite texts with more conviction. They sank to their knees with such deep and audible sighs of relief that a gentle breeze seemed to blow through the church. When Aunt Margaret slipped softly in some seconds later the air stirred with a fresh impetus.

There was only one thing that could spoil the Aunts' gladness, and that was the vox humana stop which some misguided person had presented. When its sound quivered through the air, the Aunts quivered too. Serenity faded from their faces. On Aunt Margaret the effect was particularly painful. She sighed; she drooped. If she was still kneeling she folded herself up till there seemed little of her left. Though her face was buried in her hands we knew by the trembling of her bowed body how much she was suffering. Why it was so we never understood, for to us that vox humana stop seemed intensely moving and beautiful. However, later on the organist usually kept it in reserve for the last voluntary, so that more often than not the Aunts remained undisturbed by it for nearly an hour and a half.

To the prayers they responded with a chorus of long-drawn Amens. We used to note the order of their response. Aunt Louisa, least emotional where religion was concerned, used a short sharp tone. Aunt Selina followed with deep, authoritative emphasis. Slow to assert authority in daily life, she seemed in church to adopt a commanding tone towards God. Aunt Caroline and Aunt Mary, bound together by a particular bond of tenderness, nearly synchronized. Last of all, when the vicar had already started the next prayer, Aunt Margaret breathed a long imploring A-a-men.

If we had loud-voiced Tom Merritt at home, the Aunts had the miller—the same who flung the Toll Gate open on weekdays. His singing was a source of minor discomfort to them, though it did not possess the painful potency of the vox humana stop. He sang too loud and took such a hold of his own tune that the little choir-boys often gave up the struggle with theirs. And because the church was much smaller than ours, and the Aunts were more musical, the effect on them was far more vexatious. Aunt Margaret would turn a piteous look on the face that, flour-white on weekdays, now glowed like a peony above his surplice. 'If only,' she would sigh at lunch-time, 'if only the miller would sing more softly, how happy I should be!'

Besides the miller and the vox humana stop the behaviour of the vicar sometimes caused regret. I think he must have been 'higher' than the Aunts. Possibly he bowed to the altar, or stood between them and it, I cannot remember. I only know that occasionally on the way home or at lunch-time we caught murmurs of mild disapproval.

But the Aunts were too genuinely devout to carp uncharitably. He was their minister, and they paid him the respect due to his office, and besides, they felt a certain affection for him, and he for them. When he came to tea they laid themselves out to be gracious. Aunt Mary would even be a little playful. And he humoured them. He said funny things in a crisp dry way that caused a flow of quiet laughter round the table. His voice, completely unecclesiastical, had

74

a charm and flavour all its own, and made him seem more a man of the world than any other parson we had met.

In church we were too barricaded between Aunts to look about us much, and we missed our special friends. Nor were there ever such attractive young men to be seen as our horsy farmers.

And though I am certain that in spite of occasional sighs and tightened lips the five sisters were making a genuine act of worship, I am bound to confess that their intense manner of joining in both prayers and singing had a devastating effect on our own religious feelings. More than at any other time were we conscious that our Aunts were really very peculiar.

Then when the time for the sermon came they settled themselves down with an air of complete tranquillity. Aunt Selina, indeed, nodded occasionally, and if this grew too noticeable Aunt Caroline or Aunt Mary nudged her unobtrusively.

Throughout the sermon a happy anticipation sustained us —the thought of a visit to Goaty. This absurd name—I am not sure whether I even spell it rightly—belonged to a strip of Southampton Water immediately behind the church.

Aunt Louisa knew how we loved it, and as soon as the service was over, while the other Aunts exchanged greetings with their friends, she took us there. Till we had reached the end of the churchyard we walked decorously beside her. But once we gained the field beyond, caught a glimpse of the shining water below and smelt the good salt air, the spirits that too long an ordeal had partially quenched burst into life again and down we raced, discarding all forced restraint and solemnity with shouts of joy.

Here sea-gulls, who never visited our downs in those days (they travel further now), swooped round us; here baby waves lapped at our feet, and strange salty plants, such as sea-lavender and sea-asters, grew; here, above all, a view of distant ships docked at Southampton woke all that was most adventurous in us.

If, on Sundays, reading matter and amusements were more restricted at Eling, food was unusually delectable and lavish.

The fact that the joint was cold, to spare the cook, did not worry us for we were accustomed to it at home. The potato balls, flavoured with chopped parsley, the salad with cream dressing, the excellence of the fruit tart and of the vanilla custard in little glasses more than atoned, and fortified us for a tiresome game that Aunt Caroline liked us to play with her on Sundays.

Well crammed with food, obediently we sat with her on the verandah to receive sheets of paper printed with a large clock-face, also a pencil and a Bible each.

'Today the word is Peace,' she might announce. Then began a desperate search for texts that brought in the word 'Peace'.

We admired Aunt Caroline and tried hard to please her. The game was not too difficult at first, but as longer and longer texts were needed our energy began to flag and our legs to fidget. The bright afternoon was passing. Aunt Caroline noted sadly our growing indifference, gathered together the clocks, and set us free for a walk in the Manor Woods.

After Sunday tea, which always included an iced cake, we elder ones had to make a momentous decision. Did we wish to attend evening service with the younger Aunts or stay at home with the older ones? Innocent of the pitfall that lay before me when this question was first asked, I said I would like to stay at home. I thought of the row of Anne Pratt flower-books in the dining-room. With Aunt Louisa safely

76

out of the way I would enjoy a glorious hour among them. I found myself sadly mistaken.

No sooner had the others set out for church than Aunt Selina and Aunt Margaret appeared with Bibles and prayer-books. My heart sank, but still I hoped that perhaps I might not be involved. So I stole away to the further end of the verandah. Aunt Selina's voice recalled me. 'We are going to have our Sunday evening reading now, my dear, and would like you to join us.'

Resistance was vain. Somehow we could not resist the Aunts. They were never unkind, rarely stern, but the pressure exerted by five people all armed by an unshakable conviction of what was right and what wrong, was too much for us. We submitted passively on nearly every occasion.

So now I hid my disappointment as best I could and sat down between the Aunts. Here I should say that these two rarely quarrelled on Sundays and that was why Aunt Caroline could safely leave them alone. First there was a psalm read by the three of us, verse by verse. This was followed by a portion from the New Testament. It never occurred to the Aunts to be selective in their choice where a child was concerned. The evening lesson must be read, and nothing else. On this occasion it must have been from the Epistle to the Romans, for I remember that it was all about circumcision. Circumcision . . . uncircumcision. The words recurred over and over again, and with each repetition I longed more intensely to be alone with Anne Pratt. I looked at Aunt Selina squinting down at her Bible, at her protuberant teeth that continued to grow more noticeable as she wrestled with the long ungainly word. I listened to Aunt Margaret dwelling on it lovingly as though it had some beauty of its own.

Bored and cross, I turned my eyes from my Bible and

watched a rose slowly dropping its petals in the evening sun. One, two, three, four, five. Down they fell on the floor of the verandah, reminding me of happier things. Suddenly silence fell.

'Your turn, my dear,' said Aunt Selina.

I plunged to find the place. Here was more Abraham, more circumcision.

'No! No! I've just read that!' The intensification of Aunt Selina's squint betrayed her vexation. Aunt Margaret laid her finger on the right place with a reproachful sigh. There was no escape.

Next Sunday evening I chose church.

After supper on Sunday we made our way to the big drawing-room. Bowls of pot-pourri scented the air, and the sweet smell of the furniture, impregnated through the polishing of generation after generation. Lamps with shades of rose-coloured silk threw a soft glimmer on gilded chairs, on the small chandeliers on the chimney-piece and the big ones that hung from the ceiling. Altogether the room held for us a definitely sacrosanct atmosphere.

The evening tea-tray was set on a table inlaid with squares of many-coloured marble. Even the cups were not the week-day ones, but low and wide and richly gilded. Books were never read in the drawing-room, and few kept there. Only albums with padded leather covers lay about on small tables. Aunt Margaret would open one filled with my grandmother's drawings. 'Look at her fine, beautiful lines,' she would say reverently. To us, who learned from our village schoolmaster to draw largely and boldly, these sketches seemed too faint and too 'squiggly'. But of course we never said so, and now I can see a beauty in them unrecognized then.

On the chimney-piece stood my grandmother's treasured drawing of Netley Abbey.

But we enjoyed the albums containing Aunt Margaret's own work best. Forbidden by our governess at home to use Chinese white, we loved and envied the strong body colours on tinted paper that we found there.

When Aunt Margaret had finished with sketchbooks, and the other Aunts had perhaps reviewed the evening sermon, Aunt Caroline would say: 'And now, dear Mary, if you are not too tired would you be so very kind as to sing to us?' Whereupon Aunt Margaret and Aunt Mary would move down the room to the grand piano. While Aunt Mary looked through her music, Aunt Margaret let her long thin fingers ripple over the keys in a most bewitching way. I have never known anyone who produced such watery ripplings as Aunt Margaret. It filled me with delicious sensations. But Aunt Mary's singing was a different affair.

She forced her notes too far forward through her wide nostrils, and she employed an amount of tremolo that made us shudder and long to rush from the room. Indeed, it had much the same effect on us as the vox humana stop had on the Aunts. Another weak point was that one never heard the words, or only now and then as though by accident. Many of her songs, moreover, were in Italian or German. But all her sisters thought Aunt Mary's singing perfect, and had so impressed this fact on us that we could only suppose ourselves utterly deficient in musical taste—as indeed we were. There was one person, however, who agreed with us and that was Jock the Pomeranian. As soon as Aunt Mary lifted up her voice he lifted his in a long melancholy wail, and if remonstrances and tender smacking failed he was taken away to the Servants' Hall.

Aunt Caroline remained convinced that he was so deeply moved by the singing that he tried to join in, and she only turned him out of the room because on no account must Aunt

79

Mary be interrupted. But we knew better. We were positive that he shared our distaste, and gave expression to it in his own way.

When my mother stayed in the house it is certain that Aunt Mary—and Aunt Caroline, with her clear, far-seeing eyes—found her expression discouraging. Those Sunday evenings would pass without any singing; and once I overheard a low dialogue between the two sisters.

'She has no taste for music at all, dear.'

'No, none, dear. You remember how she boasted that she is sure of no tunes but "God Save the King" and "Rule Britannia".'

'Your singing is wasted on her.'

'Yes, and I find it hard to sing when she is there.'

'Dear Mary. I understand. We all understand. We shall not ask you to sing tonight.'

By the time that Aunt Mary had sung two or three times her voice would begin to give out, and there arose a chorus of loving admonitions not to strain it any more, followed by a call to Aunt Margaret to play something before we all went to bed. Unaccustomed to any music at home except church music on Sundays and an occasional village concert, we were terribly ignorant on the subject. But I have an idea that she often chose a nocturne by Chopin and also Mendelssohn's 'Songs without Words'.

At all events Aunt Margaret's playing, as I have said, caused me deep satisfaction provided I did not look at her. If I did, the swaying of her body, the enraptured expression on her face under a cap always a little askew, might, I knew, prove too much for me.

She played largely from memory and loved to have the lights in the room turned low. This made it easier for her arpeggios to work their spell unspoiled by misplaced mirth.

So Sunday came to an end with more prayers, but at these the maids' presence was not required. The grand piano was covered over. The albums and sketchbooks were set back tidily on the little tables, and the lamps turned out. Our great-grandfather and great-grandmother dominated their end of the drawing-room for another week. It was very much an ancestral room. At the opposite end my grandfather, a handsome man with a benign but authoritative air, sat at his writing-table before an open window beyond which rose the spire of Salisbury Cathedral.

Below him hung a miniature of his mother, the demure little girl in the big picture, now a pale, grave woman in a close-fitting lace cap and a large lace ruffle. Two other sons kept her company. George, a romantic figure in his tight blue naval uniform, had fought against Napoleon, had been shipwrecked off the coast of Florida and had fed on dried dolphin and alligator. An endearing lock of hair hung down his forehead and there was the suggestion of a pout on his lips as if he still remembered the taste of the alligator. Beside him was his soldier brother Henry, who died young in the Peninsular War.

And tucked away half out of sight we caught sight of a faded photograph of a third uncle: Peter, elderly, good-looking, wearing a high butterfly collar, immense coat-tails, and tight, light trousers on his elegantly crossed legs.

But the Aunts, so full of pride in their father, and to a lesser extent in George and Henry, showed none at all in Peter.

V

Family Background

Children are seldom deeply interested in the past, and this was certainly true of ourselves. Had we been so we could have drawn from the Aunts a fund of information about our ancestors.

Still at odd times—in the drawing-room on Sunday evenings, when any but insufferably dull story-books were taboo, or during visits to the Aunts in their bedrooms—we did gather enough to fashion a rough history of those people whose painted faces were so familiar to us; a history supplemented by odd scraps of information from my father and the reading of a few extracts from old diaries.

It seemed that our great-grandmother, Selina, who, as a minute girl in a long white dress and absurd black mantilla, looked at us from one end of the drawing-room behind her mother's billowing skirts, was left an orphan at the age of nineteen. Then for three years she lived with her mother's family, the Bathursts, at Clarendon Park in South Wiltshire, till in 1782 she married my great-grandfather, William Hony, vicar of Liskeard, a Cornish 'squarson' who owned the living, as well as considerable farm-lands in the neighbouring parish of Menheniot.

My father, who inherited these lands, took us once to Liskeard, and then through deep lanes full of primroses twice the size of our little Wiltshire ones, up a road carved through the rock to the grey-stone, hill-top village of Menheniot. We could not visit the old home of the Honys because it had been burnt down nearly a hundred years before. My father, who took us to Cornwall for all our holidays, shared *his* father's deep love for the county. But Selina, who had exchanged a richly-wooded countryside and a gay, luxurious life for a remote little Cornish town far from her relations and friends, cherished no affection for it. Not that in any case, wherever she lived, she would have had much time for gaiety, with ten children arriving in quick succession during the thirteen years before her husband died and yet another on the way.

For a long while she evidently felt nostalgia for Clarendon, returned to it for long visits after her widowhood, and was distinctly peevish about Taunton, where she eventually went to live.

Her eldest son, Peter, a handsome, selfish, lively person whose faded photograph we had observed half hidden on the chimney-piece, inherited the Liskeard living but left the care of it to two ill-paid curates while he roamed Europe. Only when danger threatened his tithes, or his stables needed repair, would he tear himself from galleries and conversaziones in Paris, Rome, Naples, Milan or Seville, for a hasty stay in the great cold vicarage. And always, so he averred, the Cornish air injured his health, though, as my grandfather once dryly remarked: 'It is the lack of congenial society rather than the climate that affects Peter's health.' Wherever he went, Peter, it seems, cleverly contrived to work his way into fashionable circles.

George, the sailor on the drawing-room chimney-piece, a young man of charm, wit and courage, never wholly recovered from a 300-miles tramp after his shipwreck on the coast of Florida in 1802, on bare, lacerated feet, and tormented by hunger and thirst. Though he gained quick promotion; though he took part in many exciting naval engagements which brought him in so much prize-money that he could now snap his fingers at a niggardly guardian uncle, and talk of 'Boney' as 'the best friend the English have ever had' —in spite of all this he never regained his health after the privations he had suffered in the burning sun. Excruciating headaches plagued him for the rest of his life, and he died when only twenty-eight, leaving behind him a diary in which he had recorded his experiences in full detail. The Aunts spoke of him with pride.

Life was a dangerous affair for young men in those days. Henry, the third son, came to a pitiful end, aged twenty-one, on the retreat from Corunna. The Aunts heard from their father how passionately Henry longed to be sent to Spain, away from 'this country where people cut their throats because of the vile climate', and how impatiently he had waited for an east wind to carry him from Portsmouth. Three months later a brother officer found him sitting frozen and starved in a cart beside the road near Lugo. A mug of negus in front of a farmhouse fire came too late to save him, and he died quietly half-an-hour later. My grandfather received a letter giving all the sad details from the young officer.

In contrast to these two my grandfather, William, twin to Henry, led a quiet and sheltered life. As in the case of his brothers before him, the Cornish coach—'a regular old rattle-trap,' so he told my father—carried him off to school at Truro.

From school he went to Exeter College, Oxford, of which at the age of twenty he was made a Fellow. Later he used to speak of the low ebb of religious life at the university in those days. But admittedly this troubled him much less then than it would have later on, for when young the whole bent of his mind was towards the natural sciences, particularly botany.

He told his sisters, who passed the story on to their nieces, how with his fellow-students he used to sit round a table heaped with flowers and listen to the Professor discoursing on the one they held in their hands at the moment, and concluded: 'There is no other study that prepares the mind in equal degree for virtuous impressions.'

That in later years his wife and daughters shared his love of nature was a constant source of joy to him.

His sisters were persuaded to study botany too, and he begged them never to be led astray into preferring the flowers in milliners' shop-windows to wild flowers. At this time it seems that his two younger sisters, Harriet and Caroline, were being educated at an Establishment for Young Ladies at Exeter, and Caroline (his special favourite) told her nieces how earnest he was that she should not be content with dancing and playing on the harp, like so many girls, but that she should learn to spell correctly and write grammatically.

Geology and archaeology as well as botany strongly attracted him. During a vacation in 1809, two years before little Mary Anning unearthed her famous ichthyosaurus, he went digging for fossils near Lyme Regis. His discovery was only 'the shoulder-blade of a crocodile or some such beast', but he declared: 'I would sooner have dug out the whole skeleton than be Emperor of all the Russias.' This was apparently a favourite expression in those days. Even so, with only this one bone he was a proud and happy young man, and he sent it home on his pony and made the journey himself on foot.

During the summer vacation of 1814, when the future of Europe was in the melting-pot, he was peacefully searching for flowers in the wilds of Scotland. This was the occasion of his first sea voyage, for he decided to sail in a fishing-smack from Leith to London—a three-day journey that cost him only £4. An extra pound had enabled him to have a berth to himself.

In 1815, only a fortnight after the battle, he visited the field of Waterloo and saw grim sights that he recorded in his diary—the ground still stamped with the footprints of men and of horses, a terrible little wood full of half-buried corpses, a man's hand sticking out of the ground. With deep relief he returned to Brussels for a talk with an old gentleman about geology and an examination of his fossils.

Thus, while Peter toured the Continent with his servant and his own bed, my grandfather made his way about as best he could, often on foot, sustained always by immense curiosity and enthusiasm. But a time came when holidays grew far fewer and shorter. For in 1827 he married Margaret Earle, daughter of a country parson, whom he met while dividing his time between Oxford and Great Somerton in North Oxfordshire, of which he had been made vicar.

The honeymoon, spent in France and Switzerland, was his last real fling, though later he occasionally took my father on a brief French visit. The Aunts treasured their mother's account of her honeymoon. It was the first time she had left England and her romantic raptures—'as we ascended the Jura at midnight the ice-clad slopes were shown in sublime grandeur by flashes of lightning' and so forth—might well have flowed from Aunt Margaret's pen. From his honeymoon my grandfather took home the marble clock of which I have already spoken—a clock that ticked out the rest of his and his wife's lives, and still, after 135 years, ticks for his grandson.

On his marriage his college gave my grandfather the living of Baverstock in South Wiltshire, and there he stayed till his death forty-seven years later. The village lies in the

Nadder Valley some seven miles west of Salisbury. Set well off the Shaftesbury road and built haphazard along a winding lane that fades out at the foot of the downs, it was, and remains, very small, very obscure.

From the day on which he took up his residence in the pleasant vicarage facing south across wide meadows, he flung himself whole-heartedly into his new life. It was evident from all the Aunts told us that he became a devoted and dedicated parson.

Not only did he hold constant Bible classes, but he helped many men to read and he resolved that in future no child should suffer from lack of education if he could help it. He set about building a little school where he himself taught regularly, and to this he attached a bakehouse, where the girls might learn to make the same excellent bread that he ate at home.

When a bitter winter set in he at once thought of his poorer parishioners and distributed a generous amount of coal. 'Now,' he would say, 'I can enjoy my fire with the comfortable thought that others have the same pleasure.'

The Aunts remembered how in the potato famine in 1847 he gave away half his crop; and then only could he relish his own dinner.

'Comfort' and 'comfortable' seem to have been among his favourite words, and nearly always denoted a spiritual or mental state. His wife was his 'dearest comfort'; he told his children that their best letters were 'comfortable'.

My grandmother, too, was as active in the village as frequent child-bearing would allow. According to an old Baverstock inhabitant (whose father had told her of his boyhood days), Mrs Hony had a way of dropping into a cottage, giving an appreciative sniff, lifting the lid of a pot and asking: 'What's for dinner?'

Apparently the housewife never minded, though one shy man hid in the coal-shed when he saw her approach.

'The mud was fearful in our lanes when we were young,' said the Aunts. 'Great ponds gathered in them. Mother ordered herself a pair of boots lined with pig's bladder from our cobbler.'

No wonder then that when goloshes were introduced from America in 1847 she and her daughters developed a passion for them which lasted all their lives.

My grandmother's days must indeed have been strenuous, for seven children were born to her between 1828 and 1845. 'She gave us our first lessons,' the Aunts told us, 'and taught in the school as well.' Of course, only the services of faithful men-and maid-servants who stayed with the family an untold number of years made this possible.

When once my grandfather overcame the obstacle of having been an Oxford don for twenty years he turned into a most loving and understanding father, remarkably attractive to all children. His own little ones followed him from room to room, and others who had never seen him before ran straight to climb on his lap. Wherever he went to preach he always asked to meet the children alone afterwards. And he was as concerned with their health as with their moral state. Baverstock was a tangle of orchards and the children were apt to get diarrhoea from eating too many green apples. So he went round begging the mothers to stop them. One of the Aunts recalled his indignation when he returned home from such an expedition to find that in his absence a little boy had been put up the kitchen chimney by the master sweep.

Everything we heard showed how generous and all-embracing was the hospitality that flowed from Baverstock Vicarage. The farmers dined on the best round of beef that Salisbury could provide. The children played hide-and-seek and had 'High Tea' with my Aunts. The builders of the little school were richly entertained when their task was over. But all this was as nothing compared to the feast that took place on the vicarage lawn after the restoration of the church, when the entire parish was present.

Queen Victoria's coronation was also the occasion of an exceptional feast and a long and eloquent sermon of which I have a copy. In it my grandfather begs the young queen to 'cast herself down in a darkened room and confess herself dust and ashes', as an antidote to the vanity and flattery surrounding her. He followed this up with a survey of the state of England in which he declared that though the Poor must always be with us, drunkenness was the real cause of their sufferings. Weekly wages of seven shillings did not, it seems, disturb his conservative mind. But as he gradually entered more fully into the lives of his people his sermons grew more humane, even if he remained unstirred by any passion for social justice.

Besides all the village hospitality my Aunts often referred

to the dinner parties exchanged with neighbouring parsons and squires. Though, said their father, these latter were 'good fellows in their way', he obviously often found their conversation tedious, for, when he read aloud to his family the Letters of the First Earl of Malmesbury (written from Salisbury in 1771), he remarked: 'Why, he describes some of our squires exactly as they are today! At Compton P. has improved everything but himself, and at Dinton the talk is still all of sheep and oxen!' Occasional talks with Sydney Herbert came as a welcome relief.

But in spite of these strictures on Wiltshire squires my grandfather, inheriting a deep love of the land from his Cornish ancestors, took immense pride and pleasure in farming his own glebe. He loathed to see it misused, and a piece of careless work made him really angry. Even when in London on ecclesiastical affairs he sent directions home about planting potatoes or hoeing mangolds.

'One or two Alderney cows grazed in our meadows,' said the Aunts, 'and we often helped in the butter making.' Their father, ever meticulous about small details, commissioned the best turner in Oxford to make a butter-pat stamped with a bee on a piece of honeysuckle, the family crest, and this remained in use for years.

Besides his parish and farming activities my grandfather read Virgil regularly with his small sons before they went away to school. He and my grandmother suffered much when this happened. Both boys started at Rodwell, near Weymouth.

After Rodwell came Rugby for my Uncle George and Marlborough for my father—this latter choice in spite of great opposition from Uncle Peter, who wanted him to enter the navy. Such a course, he was sure, would be much more pleasing to God than 'a miserable place like Marlborough', followed by ordination. Earnest prayers were offered by the whole family before the boys left home, and in my father's case at least were badly needed. Marlborough, in these days, was a frightfully rough place. Bullies suspended terrified little boys wrapped in sheets from upper windows, or held them under water in the swimming-pool till they believed themselves drowning. Sometimes the journey across Salisbury Plain was taken in deep snow, and once the coach was held up for four hours.

When he was only fifteen tragedy befell Uncle George. He slipped from a high tree and injured his spine. It was the one great sorrow in my grandfather's life.

Long visits from her mother-in-law, attended by one or more of her three daughters, must have added to my grandmother's burdens. Selina Hony in her old age was often peevish, and expected and received much cosseting. She considered a supply of dried turtle necessary for her health, and there was agitation when hot weather turned it sour and no West Indiaman was due for another week. Turtle, jelly, and broth helped to keep her going till she was eighty-eight, when she died and was buried by my grandfather in a corner of Baverstock churchyard.

During the great railway boom of 1855 disturbing news reached the vicarage. A line was planned straight through my grandfather's water-meadows! The first shock over, he accepted the fact philosophically. What really upset him was the setting of a Sunday as the last day for acceptance of all new railway plans. Horsemen were dashing along the roads from all directions. To an ardent Lord's Day Observance man like my grandfather this seemed a dreadful desecration of the Sabbath.

But the innovation made many new things possible, especially visits to Liskeard, where he and my father breakfasted off pilchards and dined off 'good Cornish goose'. And now, of course, London became readily accessible.

My grandfather found his first railway journey there far more alarming than the one by fishing-smack some forty years earlier. Two anxious daughters saw him off. The speed was fearful, so he said—seventy-seven miles in three hours—and but for the tremendous shaking he might have supposed himself to be flying.

When he had been at Baverstock twenty years he was appointed Archdeacon of Sarum, and his life grew busier than ever. For some three months every year he left his parish in charge of a curate while he and his family migrated to Salisbury. This was a most important event in the Aunts' lives. My grandparents usually went ahead in the landau, and the girls and the maids followed in the waggonette and the dog-cart. A farm waggon had set out at sunrise with the luggage, which must have been very extensive to judge from the huge domed trunks and capacious hat-boxes with which my Aunts always travelled in later life.

They all adored Salisbury and spoke of it with deep reverence. After Baverstock it came nearer perfection than any place on earth, and indeed it must have been enchanting in those days. In his *Victorian England: Portrait of an Age*, G. M. Young wrote: 'I can see the world turning wistfully in imagination . . . to the English landscape as it was, and can be no more, but of which some memorials remain with us today, in the garden at Kelmscot, in the wilder valleys of the Cotswolds, in that walled Close, where all the pride and piety, the peace and beauty of a vanished world, seem to have made their home under the spire of St Mary of Salisbury.'

The Honys occupied the South Canonry, now the Bishop's house, a roomy, friendly, eighteenth-century building, backed by a lawn dropping gently to the river, which

sometimes rose till it almost reached the walls. From the Canonry radiated endless activity. My grandfather often preached in the Cathedral as well as at Baverstock and at two other villages temporarily in his charge. He organized days of fasting and humiliation, including one in 1849, during a bad outbreak of cholera, and in 1871 a collection of money and wheat for the suffering people of Paris. Quarrelling clergy met at his house to be reconciled. Sometimes, there were 'dreadful Radicals' to be entertained, but it was only my grandmother and Aunts who minded that.

Occasionally my grandfather drove to Oxford for an important event, such as a discussion of Darwin's new book. In answer to Mr Darwin and his followers, Mr Temple (later the Archbishop) took up a more liberal position than my grandfather could altogether approve; for the enthusiastic young archaeologist had developed into a cautious and conservative churchman, who later preached in the Cathedral 'with some comfort' on the text 'I am wonderfully and fearfully made'. 'They strive to set aside the creation of man by God and substitute the gradual evolution of these wonderful bodies of ours from some sort of mollusc,' he declared. The Aunts kept a news-cutting of this sermon.

Visitations involved long and difficult journeys. The diocese was larger in those days, and my grandfather drove in his dog-cart or took the mail coach to places as far afield as Blewbury and Sonning in Berkshire.

At times the roads were so rough that he jumped from the dog-cart and took to his feet. Even in his sixties he set out on horseback across the Plain in the early morning, breakfasted at the famous 'Bustard' Inn, preached at Devizes, dined with the Wiltshire Friendly Society, and spent the night with another dynamic Wiltshire parson, Archdeacon Macdonald, vicar for nearly fifty years of Bishops Cannings.

In the course of his work he stayed with people of all sorts: one of the Peculiar People, a rich cotton manufacturer, a duke. But he never grew pompous or self-important, though sometimes he showed considerable dry humour in his comments.

For my Aunts there was much gentle gaiety—musical afternoons or evenings at the Canonry or in the garden; concerts; an occasional ball. At one period of his life my

grandfather classed these as vanities (though he refused to go as far as a brother clergyman, surely the prototype of Mr Slope, who preached vehemently against them). Fortunately for his daughters he later on changed his mind.

Life at Baverstock pursued its quiet rhythm for close on fifty years, and though my grandfather began to anticipate his death eighteen years before it took place, he worked quietly up till the end. Only when well on in his eighties did he feel that he had earned the right to refuse uncongenial engagements. Summoned to attend the Cathedral when the

Prince of Wales was to be present, he pleaded age and stayed at Baverstock.

On the forty-fifth anniversary of his wedding day he wrote a brief review of his life. 'Though the first half was happy, the last half has been happiest of all. My wife has been my eternal comfort. No one of my dear seven has ever given me one moment's cause for anxiety.' The only 'sore affliction' was George's fall from the tree. 'My dear girls, copying their mother, spend their time alleviating misery and promoting happiness. Reflecting on these mercies makes my heart overflow with gratitude.'

The fact that none of his daughters married never seems to have worried him. As he sat in his study at Baverstock looking out over lilacs and laburnums in full flower to the meadows beyond, he ended: 'It is all so beautiful. When I reflect how soon my loved ones may be expelled from this Paradise I regret I have made no effort to secure it for them.'

His physical powers decreased but not his mental ones. When in residence he still preached in the Cathedral, but if it were someone else's turn he retired into the recesses of a high box-pew with a packet of sandwiches and half a bottle of port. Of course, no Aunt ever breathed a word of this. I learned it long after from Dora Robertson's *Sarum Close*.

My grandfather died at Salisbury, in 1875, in his eighty-seventh year. He had once declared that if his wife were to be buried at John o' Groats and himself at Land's End it would not cause him a moment's uneasiness. Whether he thought the same in his old age I don't know, but certainly such an idea would have horrified the Aunts.

They buried him at Baverstock in the same shady corner of the churchyard where his mother and sisters had preceded him.

His brother Peter, now ninety-two, was living in London, comfortable and self-absorbed as ever, and still able to enjoy sherry, marsala, hock, brandy and a little champagne, of which he had recently ordered fresh supplies. Not long before his own death my grandfather sent his brother a Christmas card wishing him 'present happiness and future glory'. Did he not find this hard to believe in ? Or did that deep-rooted Victorian respect for the head of the family prevent him from passing judgment?

At all events there could be no mistake about the love and admiration universally felt for my grandfather himself. The Aunts spoke much of it and told of the tributes that poured in from people in all walks of life. I used to fancy that they exaggerated a bit until I heard an unexpected tribute to him only three years ago—over eighty years after his death. I had been wandering round the Baverstock countryside when, outside Dinton church, I met an old man who asked if I belonged to these parts. No, I said, but my grandfather had been vicar of Baverstock. He looked at me hard.

'What was his name ?' he asked.

'Hony,' I answered, whereupon he took off his hat, made me a beautiful bow and shook my hand.

Though born too late to know my grandfather personally, his name, he said, had been a household word when he was a boy.

The break-up of their home added to the Aunts' sense of loss. After a few sad weeks they went to live for a short time at Lady Cross, on the edge of the New Forest, before they settled down at Eling Manor for the rest of their lives.

Though in time they grew very fond of it no place would ever compare with Baverstock. As their father had foreseen they felt expelled from Paradise.

VI

My Mother and the Aunts

Between my mother and the Aunts there was a mutual antipathy that lasted for many years. She belonged to a different world—to one that lay essentially on the other side of the Toll Gate.

Her girlhood had been spent in Parkstone in a whirl of tea parties, dinner parties, dances; theirs in the seclusion of a tiny Wiltshire village and the precincts of Salisbury Close. She was High Church; they, Protestant and Evangelical. Her face, her figure, her clothes, were the antitheses of theirs. Her eyes were bright blue, theirs of varying nondescript shades. She wore a frizzed fringe. Their hair had never known the indignity of a curl paper; except for Aunt Margaret, who also wore a fringe, no tiny strand ever found its way over their high gleaming foreheads.

My mother's bust was exceptionally well developed, something to draw attention at a glance; theirs so flat that I used to believe that their anatomy must be entirely different. With her ample bust went a well-defined waist which for my father, unused to waists, constituted one of her special charms. The sight of her great black whalebone stays is one of my earliest recollections. The Aunts, I used to think, could never have worn anything more than Liberty bodices. They had the flattest of backs and no bulging below the belt.

Aunt Caroline it is true—and it seemed fitting in one who presided over the store-cupboard, and ordered delicious meals—was of generous proportions, but they were not fluent like my mother's.

As we grew older we realized how far more sensible were our Aunts' waists, but we had been taught that a small waist was an absolute necessity for a well-dressed woman, so we meekly submitted to the preposterous stays in which our own young bodies were encased at far too early an age. When Aunt Selina, heroically throwing aside for once her habitual reserve, ventured a protest, she was met by the unanswerable argument that my father entirely approved. This left nothing to be said, for my father was the apple of his sisters' eyes. He could do no wrong. Aunt Selina's mouth twitched convulsively, as it always did on the rare occasions when she was much moved; she withdrew, a beaten woman.

Whereas the Aunts wore dresses of sober hue, cut always in much the same fashion, in those early days at all events, my mother had a fancy for dashing and often original clothes. She applied the same technique to us. Other children sported petticoats and white drawers—we wore only knickers to match our frocks. I remember Aunt Louisa unpacking my clothes and mourning over the solitary petticoat and pair of drawers that had been included for 'a special occasion'.

Our party clothes were sometimes odd and exotic, for my mother had a passion for buying remnants at sales, and as she knew nothing about dressmaking the material was often insufficient. But she never let this defeat her. Two pieces of stuff were united. I remember feeling miserably conspicuous in a frock of cinnamon velveteen with a wide sky-blue silk yoke.

Aunt Margaret sighed deeply when she saw it. The next day she took me to the village dressmaker, and instructed her to make me a frock of dark green cashmere, to take its place. This I wore at children's tea parties as long as I stayed at the Manor. But on our return home my mother sent it to the village jumble sale.

Mutual antipathy started from the moment when my father brought his prospective bride to visit his mother and his sisters. Indeed, it began before they ever met. There was the weighty question of origins. None of my father's family had ever engaged in business. True to their type and period they had all been parsons, soldiers or sailors. But now, an awful rumour reached Eling, and one Aunt wrote to another: 'If, my dear sister, she is, as you say, an ironfounder's daughter, then it is indeed a sad state of affairs.' Actually my mother's father was a most respectable ecclesiastical architect, whose design for the Albert Memorial, so she used to tell us with pride, came second to the winning entry. That surely should have carried weight with the Aunts.

But, origins apart, the news of my father's engagement dealt a blow to their hopes. Their elder brother had married a general's daughter, a good woman and a very dear one. Since at forty the younger remained a bachelor, pleasant plans for the future had been decided. They would take it in turns—Aunt Mary, perhaps, a longer one than the rest—to keep house for him and to help him run his parish. Now all that was over.

Even so, in spite of their disappointment, they would have been prepared to welcome a woman of their own sort, someone like their elder brother's wife. But, as I have said, my mother was of a very different type. How clearly I can imagine that first meeting. It took place in the long drawing-room with its chandeliers and the large Gainsborough family portrait. My grandmother, then about eighty, wearing her large frilled cap, is seated in the place of honour at the far

end of the room, with her five daughters grouped about her. Sounds are heard in the hall—my father's cheerful voice speaking to Matilda, the tap of my mother's high heels. The door opens and in front of the portrait of our elegant and slightly haughty great-great-grandmother, her husband and daughter, stands the young woman from Parkstone, in a dress that accentuates her flowing curves. A fashionable little hat is tipped over her bright eyes, her cheeks are rosy but quite unblushing. My father puts his arm round the waist that he finds so beautiful, and leads her forward. She is completely at ease, quite undaunted.

The Aunts wilt at sight of her. This is far worse than they had imagined, and, what is more, they recognize at once that here is someone whom they will be unable to mould to their pattern. Her own is far too clearly defined already. They had thought to impress her with the dignity of their family, to make her feel what an honour they are conferring upon her when they receive her into it. But she is not impressed. It may even be that there is a sparkle of mischief in her eyes as she shakes hands with her future sisters-in-law, and finds each one plainer than the last. Moreover, they are 'old maids', and for that genus my mother feels all the opprobrium customary to her time. As to what they think of *her*, she does not care twopence. Aunt Margaret may sigh softly, Aunt Selina's mouth tighten and loosen, Aunt Louisa throw her little nose in the air, Aunt Mary flutter her hands under the ruffles at her wrist—it is all one to her. Only Aunt Caroline, gazing at her with that peculiarly straight look that had such power to discomfort us when we knew ourselves guilty of some small misdemeanour, commands her unwilling respect. And to my old grandmother, I feel sure, she is gracious and even possibly a little humble.

Relations remained strained and difficult for many years.

In fact they never grew entirely easy. As children, even without my mother's frequent rather caustic comments when
we were alone with her, we scented the hostility in the air.

The sense of divided loyalties often made things difficult
for us. At home we accepted my mother's judgments un-
questioningly, but when we went to Eling and found ourselves lapped round by kindness, we often forgot that they
were old maids, ridiculously old-fashioned, narrow-minded
—that Aunt Louisa was inquisitive, Aunt Mary kittenish,
and all the rest of it. And especially was this the case when,
as usually happened, we stayed alone with them. If my
parents accompanied us there were sometimes extremely
difficult moments. My father tried hard to smooth them over,
and often succeeded, but once a storm arose beyond even his
control. Its cause was insignificant—the colour of my
mother's hair.

One evening while Aunt Louisa was putting us to bed she
remarked as she brushed ours, that it was very pretty. 'It is
dark on your heads,' she said, 'but golden at the ends.'

'Mother's hair is like that too,' we told her.

Aunt Louisa answered darkly: 'Ah! But some people put
something on their hair to make it so.'

Little fools that we were, we repeated this conversation to
my mother.

Her mouth tightened with anger. 'She dared to say that!'
she cried.

When we saw the effect of our words we wished we had
held our tongues. Still more did we wish it next day. Suddenly, in the middle of lunch, after the maids had left the
room, we heard my mother address Aunt Louisa in a loud
voice from the opposite side of the table.

'Louisa,' she said, 'how dare you tell the children that I
dye my hair?'

It was as though a thunderbolt had dropped through the ceiling. I felt myself trembling violently. Complete silence reigned for a moment, before Aunt Louisa, dazed by the attack, could answer: 'I didn't—I didn't!' And then she began to sob. She was easily reduced to tears.

'Yes, you did,' continued my mother relentlessly; 'the children always speak the truth. You told them that I put stuff on my hair to make the ends a different colour.'

'Annie, Annie, hush!' entreated my father.

It was too late. The whole table was in a tumult. Aunt Louisa's tears were pouring into her soup. The other Aunts gazed with indignation at my mother. My sister and I longed to slip under the table out of sight. Then Aunt Caroline rose from her place and went to her afflicted sister.

'Come, dear,' she said in a low voice and led her from the room. I can still see Aunt Louisa's thin body shaken by sobs as she went. All my feeling was now for her. My sister and I were a pair of Judases. It was we who were responsible for this terrible scene. Yet I do not remember that anyone blamed us, not even Aunt Caroline. Later she said to us, quite gently: 'Dear Aunt Louisa has a weak heart. We must always try not to disturb or hurt her.'

My mother remained unmoved. She was sure she had taken the right action at the right time. It may be that later she repented, but not then. The meal continued in constrained silence and it was with difficulty that we swallowed our food.

Later, the antipathy felt on both sides mercifully lessened. My mother, recognizing their unfailing kindness, and that they were good women (apart from some hypocrisy), grew more tolerant both of her sisters-in-law and of their oddities. They, in their turn, were forced to realize that, in spite of, for them, certain objectionable characteristics, she made their brother extremely happy and was a good mother—on the whole.

I only wish that this better understanding could have been reached earlier for everybody's sake.

VII

Change and Decay

The years passed, their monotony only broken by such a grievous event as the death of Aunt Louisa or, in a different category, by the demands made by Lloyd George's Insurance Act and similar political catastrophes.

With the growing-up of the nephews and nieces visits to the Aunts were no longer undertaken in bulk. We went separately as work or education allowed. The outbreak of World War I caused a further limitation. In the early disastrous days, when I went to Eling from London for a few days' holiday, Aunt Caroline and Aunt Mary met me at the station with mysterious looks. It was evident that they possessed a secret which they were dying to unfold.

Before they had driven far Aunt Caroline, after glancing carefully round to make sure that no passer-by could hear, leaned forward and said in a low voice:

'My dear, though things look so black, we have news to comfort you. The station-master drew us aside while we were waiting and told us that train-loads of Russians were passing along the line all through the night——'

'The blinds were drawn,' Aunt Mary broke in on a whisper, 'so that nobody should see them, because it is of the utmost importance that the enemy shall be kept completely in the dark.'

'You understand, my dear?' Aunt Caroline picked her up. 'You must not breathe one word of this till it becomes common knowledge.'

I was deeply impressed and promised to treat this astonishing piece of news with the utmost secrecy.

Though the war naturally made an extreme emotional impact on the Aunts and coloured much of their conversation; though Aunt Selina and Aunt Margaret fought for the morning paper; yet it could not seriously alter the Daily Round. Only now, instead of knitting for the Esquimaux, the two younger Aunts worked tirelessly at vast blue scarves or Balaclava helmets for sailors. Aunt Margaret tried to appear excessively busy with some khaki wool, but since she dropped nearly as many stitches as she knitted and had to be constantly rescued by a younger sister, I am afraid that no member of the forces ever went the warmer for her efforts.

Aunt Selina, entrenched behind *The Times*, either dozing or reading laboriously with constant movements of her lips, did not even try to knit.

One day the household was thrown into a flutter by news that two officers were to be billeted on them for a few days. Some years later I happened to meet one of these young men. He drew a vivid picture of the arrival of himself and his companion, travel-stained and tired, on an autumn evening.

'We were shown at once into the drawing-room,' he said, 'and from the far end, in the dim light, four old ladies rose from their chairs with a rustle of silk and lace; they moved forward one by one to welcome us in the most courtly manner. Throughout our visit they treated us as honoured guests, and gave us vintage port from their cellar every night. I made special headway with Aunt Margaret because I too am by way of being an artist. I stood reverently with her before the Gainsborough.'

'Did she take you to see "The Wings of the Morning"?'

'Yes. I told her it reminded me of Turner and she said with tears in her eyes that I had so encouraged her that she would now try to finish it, though of course the war made it very difficult for her.'

'She never finished it.'

'No. I knew she never would. She was too old and blind. The whole of our visit was a unique experience. Your Aunts took us back fifty years. As we sat in the drawing-room under the chandeliers and listened to Aunt Margaret playing Mendelssohn it was hard to believe that half the world was at war.'

Yet almost imperceptibly the Aunts, their men-servants and their maid-servants, their domain, were changing.

Walking to church became an ever more difficult problem, till at last after earnest consultation with Beech and their own consciences the victoria and one white horse would appear at the front door to take Aunt Selina and Aunt Margaret. Later, these two gradually ceased to struggle down to morning prayers and had their breakfast in bed. In the studio dust and solitude reigned. Aunt Selina, after further falls, was forbidden to climb on chairs. Rheumatism increasingly hampered Aunt Caroline and stopped her from keeping a dog.

Only Aunt Mary remained active and comparatively youthful. Alone among them she tried valiantly to move with the times. By then I had married a doctor—much interested in the treatment of nervous troubles—and in spite of objections from her elder sisters that it was a most dangerous thing to allow, she even asked him to treat by suggestion a favourite village protégé who suffered from constant headaches.

She too was the only one who accepted the doctor as an equal, even though she shared with her sisters the terrible suspicion that he might be related to their fishmonger because he bore the same uncommon name. When I went alone on a visit I asked if I might be driven into Southampton to visit an old uncle of my husband's. There was a frigid silence and an exchange of meaning looks across the table, followed by some paltry excuse from Aunt Caroline. Beech was too busy, the horses could not be spared. It was not till some time later that the real reason transpired.

As it happened the uncle was an Angel; an Angel of that strange little body, the Catholic Apostolic Church. Would that have been better than kinship to a fish-monger, I wondered?

Beech himself began to wear a look of chronic discontent, which had a double origin. To begin with he felt himself an anachronism. From time to time the Aunts dropped vague hints that they might give up the horses, buy a car, and let him learn to drive. But always they shied away from the final decision. As long as Hazel and Walnut, snow-white now and very plump, could lollop gently as far as Southampton Aunt Caroline opposed the change. And Beech saw himself in a cul-de-sac from which he would never emerge. Nor was this his only trouble. The Aunts, so generous in many ways, entirely failed to grasp current economic trends. So Beech and White were paid much the same wages as they had received for twenty years. Week by week Beech's green coat with the brass buttons grew shabbier and tighter. It was a wonder that he ever troubled to polish the buttons, and still more of a wonder that he never protested about his pay.

White, too, wore clothes that would have been more suit-able for a scarecrow. He continued to supply the house with a wealth of vegetables and fruit—melons and grapes, peaches and nectarines, as well as homelier things, but there was a dispirited droop to his shoulders, and he rarely smiled. The beard that had once reminded us of moss, now seemed like lichen on an old tree stump. His sole assistant in the big garden was a man even more ancient than himself.

The lawns grew progressively spongier and moister, and the dead leaves, unswept, gathered in deep drifts under the remoter trees. Roses went unpruned. Only the flower-beds just outside the verandah still flaunted their red, white and blue. White had long given up the struggle with calceolarias and begonias.

Inside the house, Matilda grew stouter and redder and slower in her movements, but retained her patience and her kindliness. Elizabeth had deserted some years previously, unable any longer to endure being one of a household of spinsters. Her place was filled by a gentle, patient old body who accepted orders with a meekness neither of the other two had ever shown.

After the war there were no more trips abroad and few to Southampton. But if any of us came to stay we still drove with Aunt Mary along the road to the Forest, to the obvious enjoyment of passing motorists, who slowed down for a good look at us: at the melancholy coachman in his shabby coat; the fat, slow-trotting horse (Walnut was dead now, and Hazel 33 years old); the aged lady in her mantle of black silk, sheltering under her parasol from the sun and vulgar curiosity.

As age pressed heavily on them the Aunts began examining their wardrobes with a view to passing on to their nieces, before the moth got in, such garments as they thought themselves unlikely to wear again. It was rather like capitalists handing over some of their wealth before death duties could make holes in it. When we gazed unhappily at these unsuitable clothes and muttered vague reasons why we could not wear them, the Aunts told each other in audible asides how lacking we were in good taste.

'Never mind, dear,' I heard Aunt Mary say. 'She has no sense of clothes; she dresses very badly—goes about in a coat and skirt made of that corduroy stuff that labourers wear and thinks herself smart, yet refuses your handsome silk coat.'

No other Aunt followed Aunt Louisa to the grave for nearly twenty years. Aunt Selina lived on, usually in her burrow at the end of the passage, walled in by her impenetrable reserve. During the long evenings in the Blue Room she slept continuously. Sometimes she rose to go to bed about nine o'clock, but was always gently but firmly told by Aunt Caroline or Aunt Mary to wait till ten o'clock for prayers.

The manner of her dying at ninety-six, following a stroke, was typical of her staunch conservatism and her groping after God. She would ask for *The Times* to be brought in and then hold it up before her, but, though her lips moved, it is doubtful whether she took in a single word. After a couple of minutes she would drop the paper and break into a quavering line or two of 'Abide with me', and then return to *The Times*. In a little while she died as unobtrusively as she had lived. She had been but half alive for so long that only the empty chair and the empty room in the far corner of the house testified to her absence.

I have already spoken of the sad change that gradually came over Aunt Margaret. As old age closed in, her lovable qualities continued to dwindle and her less pleasing ones to intensify. Once she had been genuinely moved by beauty; now she only pretended to be. Once her sighs had expressed real emotion at the trend of affairs or at the sufferings of others. Now she sighed for herself alone. As for Aunt Caroline and Aunt Mary, they had to draw on all their stock of patience and remembered affection during her last years. She was ninety-three when she died.

Aunt Caroline was the next to go. For over a year she

superintended the household from her bed, holding the reins firmly in her hand, keeping her clear mind and her searching gaze to the last, linked to Aunt Mary by a bond that grew closer and closer. Anxious to save her sister trouble, and to ensure that they would lie side by side, she chose burial in Eling churchyard instead of at Baverstock.

And so at last the youngest sister was left alone, a forlorn little figure in the big house. At first she planned to leave it and spend the remainder of her life in Salisbury. But the prospect of such an upheaval proved too much for her, and she stayed on with the three maids and Beech and White. Hazel still drew her along the road to the Forest, or sometimes even beyond the Toll Gate.

Though this continued to act as a partial barrier against the ever increasing outflow from Southampton, an insidious invasion was taking place all the time in the quiet meadows that lay south of the Manor. A new road was made. Rows of little red-brick houses sprang up. Aunt Mary, looking out over the rhododendron hedge from an upper window, saw all too clearly the dreaded enemy, urbanization, creeping closer and closer. But she would not allow this or anything else to embitter her. Uncharitable words rarely passed her lips. Though the doings of the young might puzzle her she seldom condemned them. Almost up to the day of her death she continued to visit the nearer cottages, and though often no doubt her ministrations may have seemed a little absurd, they were prompted by genuine Christian charity.

She missed Aunt Caroline terribly and was often lonely, but she retained her serenity, though at times she worried over the vast accumulation of things that filled wardrobes, drawers, boxes, and ottomans. Once on a wet day she took me upstairs to an empty room and kneeling before one of the many ottomans drew out an armful of the countless pieces of unfinished needlework that she and the others had piled up through the years. There were embroidered cushion covers, brush-and-comb bags, hair-tidys, nightdress cases, tea-cloths, tray-cloths—every kind of article that had seemed appropriate for embroidery; wrapped up inside them were the skeins of many-coloured wools and silks needed for their completion.

For a moment Aunt Mary held a cushion cover half decorated in shades of red and yellow and brown, and gazed at it consideringly.

'Dear Aunt Caroline, I remember, chose those shades after a day in the Forest,' she murmured. 'I wonder if I could finish it?'

But she did not want an answer. She knew that it was too late. Her fingers had lost their cunning, her eyes had grown dim. With a sigh she put it back in the ottoman, and said: 'Let us go back to the Blue Room, my dear.'

After five years of patient solitude the gates at the end of the drive opened and closed for the last of the Aunts.

When I went to the Manor after Aunt Mary's death it seemed impossible to believe that none of the familiar figures would ever again come down the white steps with welcoming faces, or dispense tea on the verandah, or show us the treasures in their rooms, would ever again kneel solemnly in the dining-room for morning prayers or gather themselves together for church—so much had these things and a hundred others become part of our consciousness. Aunt Selina was surely still lurking at the end of the passage; Aunt Margaret pretending to be busy in the studio; Aunt Caroline holding earnest discussion with the cook; Aunt Louisa waiting to dart out on us from behind the rhododendrons; Aunt Mary returning from the village with an empty basket. Only Matilda remained and she, after fifty years of faithful service, found herself completely adrift in spite of an adequate annuity.

As I sat on the sunny verandah, sweet as ever with the scent of the myrtles, where we had once been so happy, the Aunts' absurdities, their unconscious hypocrisies, their ridiculous snobberies, were forgotten in a sudden overwhelming recognition of all the kindness and affection that they had lavished on us.

VIII

A Backward Look

After the break-up of the old family home following Aunt Mary's death someone handed over to me a few auntly garments for my dressing-up box, and four shoe-boxes tightly packed with letters. The garments—a dress of faded blue-and-pink delaine belonging to the 'fifties, a lilac satin covered with black lace that Aunt Mary used to wear when my father came to stay, a battered straw hat with blue ribbons, a Sunday bonnet, and a moth-eaten sealskin jacket that I dimly remembered on Aunt Margaret in church—played a part in many of my children's charades.

But somehow courage failed whenever I looked at the shoe-boxes. I put them away in a dark cupboard and decided to forget them, at least for the present. Yet now and then they drew me unwillingly. I would lift a lid, untie the pink tape from one of the bundles of letters, glance uneasily at the yellowing notepaper and the thin spidery writing, then hastily re-tie the bundle, return the box to the cupboard and decide that life was too short to answer the challenge.

The years slipped by and still the challenge remained unanswered, though my five Aunts always stayed very clear in my mind, the more so because my children loved to hear about them. My eldest son would proudly tell how he had driven as a very small boy with Aunt Mary in her victoria

drawn by a white horse, of immense age, along the high road
to Lyndhurst.

Then as I grew older I found myself wanting to know
more of my Aunts' youth. Finally I took the desperate
decision to examine the boxes thoroughly.

The first bundle contained a few letters from my great-
grandmother Earle to her sister Anne, written in the year of
Waterloo.

'Indeed and indeed you are going on very gayly—however I hope it may be All in favour of poor Swerford' (the
Earles lived at Swerford in North Oxfordshire) 'for though
Novelty has always Charms, its Sober-sided pleasures must
please by and by. Here, too, it seems we are to step from the
path of Regular Routine. The Card for How Ball has arrived
. . . Colonel Dawkins is to arrive fresh from Paris for the
Occasion so we may expect some first-rate *Conduct*. I hope it
is the fashion in France to get Ladies Partners. How has not
been reported very famous for that.'

Fascinated, I read on to the end, where the writer describes her last coach journey.

'Give me such a Stage Coach as Robarts. Of All Modes I
have tried I have found none that suited me better. The
Coach carries but four—therefore we had only one more
than our own Party, and that a very Neat intelligent Woman
of London . . . Looking again I said, I surely do know your
Face—Aye, and I know yours, said she. For who should I,
that never went in a coach before, meet with but my old
friend Mrs Weston, the late Rector of Witney's Wife that I
had not seen for 22 years . . . You would have been struck to
hear me in full Prattle all the way.'

Grandmother Earle was a livelier correspondent than
Grandmother Selina Hony had ever been. These letters,
with their strong Jane Austen flavour, were delightful, but

did not help me to learn more about the Aunts, though another letter, describing great-aunt Anne, gave an amusing pre-view of Aunt Margaret.

'Her time flows on in such pleasing serenity that the evening arrives and she is too late for the Post ere the morning appears to have passed.'

How often had I seen my own aunt hurrying downstairs, her lace cap even more awry than usual, with a bunch of letters in her hand and a bewildered look on her face and heard Aunt Carry proclaim from the hall: 'Too late, dear!'

I plunged into a second box and drew out a minute sheet of paper covered with huge childish hand-writing.

'I have gone into Aprons now,' it said. 'I have gone into them several weeks. I am quite well, which is a great Comfort.

Your affectionate Chicken,
Mary'

Here was an early hint of my youngest Aunt's emphasis on her youth; here, too, one of the key-words to life at Eling: *comfort.*

The next letter, from a great-aunt, described my Aunt Caroline on a visit to Weymouth.

'The sweet child, after watching the moon shining and dancing on the water, exclaimed, "I should like to walk on the beauty Moon Sea!" '—an unexpected glimpse of my most solid, most matter-of-fact Aunt.

I decided to go ahead with my task, and I stuck to it even though, as I proceeded, the amount of space given over to rain, wind and frost, to headaches and colds, was often discouraging.

The colds were appalling. By the time I had read some 400 letters I seemed to see an unending row of clothes-baskets filled with wet handkerchiefs. Yet somehow the dullest letters helped me to build a background for the Aunts, and to understand better what made them turn into the funny old ladies whom we knew at Eling—though of course much of their lives remained unrevealed, since these letters formed only a small part of the vast correspondence left behind.

I will begin with those about Aunt Selina. We had often puzzled over why she buried herself so much in her little den, why we heard her laugh so rarely, why she always seemed to be wrestling with God when she prayed. These early letters provided an unhappy clue. For in them I found a saddening picture of a small helpless child washed and beaten by the fierce wave of evangelism that had engulfed her mother and her aunts at this time.

Her mother, just recovered from severe illness, describes herself as 'a brand snatched from the burning', begs her sister to pray that she has not been chastised in vain, and commits to memory a favourite set of verses that run thus:

> Then since this world is vain
> And volatile and fleet,
> Why should I lay up earthly joys
> Where rust corrupts and moth destroys
> And cares and sorrows eat?
> Why fly from ill with anxious skill
> When soon this hand will freeze,
> This throbbing heart be still?

She was at this time a happy, busy young woman of twenty-eight. Not content with her own conversion she turns her anxious attention on 'little Lin', barely four years old, and talks to her of the 'heinousness of sin'. In this she is backed up by her eldest sister-in-law, then staying at Baverstock. This aunt records in her confession-book her joy at seeing 'the dear child so softened by grace for the sin of disobedience that she was overcome by tears that checked her utterance of "Forgive me, Lord, for Thy dear Son, The ills that I this day have done". . . May she be an example to her dear little sisters, and, cherished by the dews of the Spirit, become a Tree of Righteousness.'

This pious hope reminded me of how I used to liken my Aunt to a closely-clipped evergreen that bore no flowers.

The pressure continued, and on the eve of her tenth birthday her mother wrote from her bedroom to the nursery: 'I cannot close this sacred day, the eve of my dearest Lin's natal day, without a few lines of congratulation.' But unfortunately these are followed by a prayer that the love of God 'may constrain you to meet the earnest love of your Parents by increasing diligence in a desire to please them'. She speaks of cross words, bad tempers, sinful inclinations. Will her beloved Lin set a guard on herself against these? So, on her birthday morning, little Lin sits down to write a tearful answer (there are smudges on the notepaper) and she writes out a prayer in a large round hand: 'May I remember this whole day that Thou, God, seest me both in work and play. Let me be well-behaved in the nursery, schoolroom, and downstairs. May a kind, gentle, obedient temper be possessed by me during the whole of this day.'

On New Year's Eve another letter goes to the nursery: 'My first-born beloved Linnie,' it begins; 'as I love you from my heart I must deal faithfully with my Child. . . You are too occupied with yourself. I hope, therefore, that in 1839 my dearest Lin will seek that grace that will enable her to think less of herself and more of others, and remember that pretty tale in *The Vale of Tears*.'

Through this Vale little Lin herself certainly passed and perhaps because of all this talk of sin her health began to cause anxiety. 'She has been a very patient child,' wrote her mother, 'but nothing gave her any pleasure. . . She lost weight so rapidly and her pulse was so indifferent that I went to bed with a tear in my e'en. . . She reminds me of Emily Trotman's (a cousin who died young) little peaked face, and her eyes are so large. Yesterday she said to me, "Mamma, I always feel poorly now." Yet she is perfectly content.'

Clearly Lin had settled into the role of sweet little invalid, of whom too much would no longer be expected. Perhaps she saw herself, like Emily, on an early death-bed. Fortunately my grandfather gradually realized what was happening and intervened. Too many talks on sin were stopped. Admonitory letters no longer went to the nursery. When two zealous aunts wanted to make the children repeat the Lord's Prayer three times before breakfast, 'No,' said he firmly, 'I will not have my children turned into Formalists.' But though the tide of evangelism died down it had undoubtedly buffeted my eldest Aunt far too hard.

Later she gardened with the same fierce energy that consumed her as she prayed, for her mother wrote to her: 'Pray do not make yourself hot and tired with planting flowers. We will work together all the merrier when I return.'

It is hard to imagine Aunt Selina ever gardening merrily. If she loved flowers she never showed it. When Aunt Margaret wrote so typically: 'So my dear lilies are in bloom! Who will kiss them for me? Mother must. She will do it so prettily,' or: 'The water-lilies are spreading their white flowers on their wide green leaves like poetic thoughts on very white wings,' Aunt Selina's mouth would have twitched most justifiably as this was read aloud at breakfast.

But she must have written things in letters that she would

never have spoken. 'Your valued letters have sweetened our breakfast table,' wrote her mother, 'together with the adjunct of Mr Sims' honey-comb.'

George's letters from Rugby, on the other hand, can hardly have had a sweetening effect:

'A man came here this week to walk, run, and do a great many things very fast, and a great many people came to see him. One man got drunk and kicked his wife and killed a baby that was in her arms. A mad dog bit a man and he died, and one man was killed at the railway station, so it was a bad week on the whole.' But perhaps another of his letters pleased them because of their animosity for the person described: 'Cardinal Wiseman preached at the Chapple yesterday, only he had a bad cold. His sermon was one and a half hours. He is a short, round-faced man and very fat. He was dressed in scarlet silk and looked like an old woman.'

To return to Aunt Selina. While young men make fleeting appearances beside the other sisters never a one crops up in her company. In two things, however, she evidently excelled. Taut as a well-sprung bow herself she was a skilled archer who won many prizes, including a pair of glove stretchers, for a 'gold' scored at Wilton House.

And though at least two of her sisters played the harp she was the one chosen to perform at village concerts in aid of Shipwrecked Mariners and other deserving causes.

As a young girl she wrote home: 'Aunt Harriet is playing most charmingly on the harp. You can't think how it makes me long to touch it.'

Soon afterwards she sold her concertina and bought one for herself.

Both because she was such a prolific letter-writer and also far less reserved than her sisters, it is Aunt Margaret whose personality shines out most clearly in the letters. And from

them I learned much of how the family dressed themselves. Clothes interested her immensely and play an important part in her correspondence. She studied the fashions closely and constituted herself the family's arbiter in matters of taste. Selina is told not to wear pink or blue 'which make your complexion appear sallow'.

'Put a camellia from the garden in your bonnet,' she advises her on a special occasion, 'and ask Aunt to lend you either a white Shetland or a black lace shawl.'

Another time, she wrote: 'I have very pretty bonnets in my head from Paris, and if you want a summer one I will gladly make it.' She loved to get lots of bonnets on approval from Thomas Bloom, the most distinguished of Salisbury drapers, and she asked them to repeat 'my dear old Cleopatra hat, but not turned down, and bound with black velvet'.

Of course it was she who planned the toilets worn for the archery contest at Wilton. Her mother, who sat in state under a cedar tree and presented the prizes, wore 'a darkish buff camlet trimmed with broad bands of black mohair' because it was 'so lady-like looking'. Selina, the heroine of the day, grappled with her bow in a black lace shawl and a bonnet trimmed with black lace and cherries. Carry and Mary wore French cashmere paletots and bonnets of white lace and pink crêpe. Margaret herself needed a 'Dolly Varden' to shade her sensitive eyes, and a dress of 'soft poppy green silk', from her favourite London shop, Howell and James. Louisa's clothes are not mentioned. I have an idea that she turned up her sharp little nose at many of her sister's ideas about dress.

It seemed entirely right when I read that Aunt Margaret hated stays. 'She suffers torment from her new stays,' wrote my grandfather, when he intervened on her behalf. In this he was in direct contrast to *my* father.

Two memorable events in Aunt Margaret's early life happened when she was on one of the many visits that the sisters paid their aunts. On both occasions the aunt was their mother's sister, Anne, who had become a pernickety lady and caused her nieces much trouble.

She chose Margaret to stay with her in Guernsey, and, as usual, many things went wrong. She herself had been extra tiresome, she disliked the people at the hotel, had insisted on having all meals in her own room, and thought the shops poor and the weather abominable. But one thing sustained her niece: the prospect of a visit to Sark, for which she confessed a romantic longing.

As in the case of Mrs Ramsey planning to go to the lighthouse, one frustration succeeded another. First it rained. Next, not enough passengers turned up so the boat did not start. Then Aunt Anne was in the wrong mood. Then she had a headache. But at last the little steamer carried them to the island of which Aunt Margaret had dreamed so long. As she gazed at the sunrise over the sea from her bedroom window she was flooded with emotion and also with inspiration for the picture before which as children we stood tongue-tied—the famous 'Wings of the Morning'.

A second visit to Aunt Anne, this time at her Wokingham home, brought only a broken romance. Margaret had gone to stay with her for Ascot, and had planned her clothes with particular care. Unfortunately her brother George, whose judgment was always accepted as final, pronounced the bonnet from Bloom's 'vulgar'.

Sad but submissive, she returned it and bought 'a shape that I have trimmed with red lilac crêpe to match my dress—that mauve muslin that Aunt gave me last year—and I shall wear a quite plain white burnous with it'.

Feeling happy and well-dressed, she set off with her Aunt

Anne in the victoria for the races. The crowd was rather frightening but George was there with some friends, and they saw 'the lovely young Princess of Wales', and also noted that the Queen 'arrived in a closed carriage and was not much cheered'.

But far more momentous to Aunt Margaret than the presence of royalty was that of Mr H., a young man who had shown her some attention the previous summer at Baverstock. One day when she and her sisters were haymaking news came that he had been seen walking down the lane towards the vicarage. Long afterwards a small cousin recounted the hurried consultation that took place and how, as a result, Aunt Margaret slipped away to change her hat. As I have related when speaking of Aunt Louisa, my Aunts believed that they never showed to better advantage than in the hayfield.

It is true that the hat seemed to have no immediate effect, but now here was Mr H. again. He came up to the carriage and 'chatted most affably', went back to his companions but returned soon afterwards. The next day they went to Ascot again, and again Mr H. joined them, and seemed so attentive that Aunt Anne asked him to play croquet on the following Sunday.

Now begins the sad part of the story. He arrived early and my Aunt took him for a turn in the garden and unburdened herself of a secret sorrow. She reminded him of two little sketches that she had sent him in gratitude for the kindness he had shown her previously. Yes, he said, they had pleased him much.

'But,' confided my Aunt, 'your sisters expressed annoyance with me for sending them, and this distressed me.'

'You are too sensitive,' replied Mr H. 'There must have been some misunderstanding.'

'No, no,' said my Aunt, 'the annoyance was twice repeated. But please never mention this to your sisters.'

By this time the other guests were arriving and the conversation broke off. During the game of croquet everything became easy and pleasant again, but when Mr H. was about to leave Aunt Margaret must needs waylay him and beg him once more to say nothing to his sisters. Her intensity over the affair was clearly too much for the young man. He answered her coldly, went his way, and was not heard of again.

'If only I had held my tongue. . . If only dear George had been here to advise me. . . Dear Mamma, I felt I must tell you the whole story.' So ends the long unhappy letter.

If only . . . if only. The words spring to mind so often where Aunt Margaret is concerned. Perhaps she cherished a dim hope that she might meet Mr H. at Ascot the following year, for she wrote to Aunt Selina: 'We think the costume of grey and pink will be very pretty for you, and though one does not want to be *smart* it is essential to be dressed like a Lady for Ascot, and you will want to look nice with George. If only Aunt had asked me, as she used to generally . . .' but Aunt Anne was contrary once more and failed to invite her.

Deep emotions stirred Aunt Margaret constantly, over public as well as private affairs. Staying in the Pays de Vaud, she rhapsodized to her mother about 'the unfenced pastures full of the most wondrous flowers', about 'the gentle cows wearing harmonious bells', about 'the soft musical voices of the inhabitants'.

Then suddenly a piece of news from England threw her into a fever of excitement—a rumour that the Arch Enemy, Gladstone, had fallen! 'It made my heart beat fast. Surely it is too good to be true!'

Her father, so much wiser and more balanced in his judgment, refused to join an attempt to oust Gladstone from the Chancellorship of Oxford University.

It is not to be wondered at that Aunt Margaret's headaches excelled everybody else's. All the family were prone to them, and they were looked on as the inevitable accompaniment to a journey or to any extra excitement. Even the schoolboy brothers suffered, and as I read letter after letter concerned with them I understood why my father once, after packing for a holiday, dreamed that someone asked him: 'Did you remember to pack a headache?'

But Aunt Margaret's headaches were colossal. Once she lay three days with drawn shutters. Anything sufficed to start them off: harsh singing in church (I thought of the suffering that the vox humana stop used to cause her), the approach of a thunder-storm, a tiff with a sister. She was also the constant victim of Bile.

'Margaret needs a little discipline as to bile,' wrote her father.

When a comet was at its brightest she lay prostrate. 'How I have longed to be walking in the garden with you,' she writes to Caroline, 'but now this will never be, for it is moving two million miles each day.' And I can imagine the soft sigh that accompanied this. When an aurora flamed in the sky she was again earthbound. 'If only this odious bile were not plaguing me my thoughts would have been lifted to pure, bright dreams of heaven.'

Perhaps it was all this biliousness that helped to turn her sour in old age. Blue Pills were her only remedy. That both she and her mother and sisters (all victims of the bile, though in a minor degree) would have been better without three large meals a day and too much cream from the Alderney cows, never seems to have crossed their minds. But though this appeared stupid I found myself growing less and less censorious of Aunt Margaret and continually making allowances for her.

The whole picture that emerged was of a high-spirited, affectionate, artistic girl, as well as of an absurdly sensitive and emotional one. Undoubtedly her nervous excitability affected her health but this in its turn may have been due to the deep anxiety her mother felt before her birth—an anxiety that preceded the birth of all her babies, but more especially Margaret's. 'Hasten your coming,' she wrote to her sister Anne, 'so that I may forget you as a novelty before the hour of trial. My nerves will then be under such a strain that perfect quiet is essential.'

To soothe her my grandfather read aloud *Paradise Lost* ('the beauties of which are more scant than I imagined') and *Polynesian Researches*, which, however, tended to keep her awake because of its 'prodigious wonders'.

Aunt Louisa figures little in the letters and when she does it is usually as a rather lonely soul. In those early days Margaret and Selina were good friends: 'My own most precious Sis', writes the younger to the elder—and Aunt Carry and Aunt Mary had already developed their lifelong devotion for each other. Aunt Louisa longed to bind herself to one of them without avail. She had a rather jealous nature. Her father wrote to Selina: 'You have your cousins to admire you now. Poor Louie is much put out about it.'

As a child she was more nervous than the others. Her father relates how in Chartist days, on returning home after the burning of an old tithe barn and a couple of ricks a mile or two away, he found her 'in a very distressed condition', and sat beside her till she fell asleep. Whenever she went on a visit she was encouraged to stay as long as possible. 'But, please, dear Mamma, I must be home for the haymaking,' she wrote pleadingly.

A bad attack of rheumatic fever was probably the cause of Aunt Louisa's later heart trouble. Forty leeches were laid on her as well as blisters, a treatment that left her very low. The doctor ordered a generous diet and plenty of wine.

Aunt Carry stands out consistently as the same solid figure, physically and mentally, that we knew so well. Her father wrote of her: 'Dear Carrie, she is my pet. . . Such a sweet-tempered sober-minded girl.' When she was only twelve he deputed her to superintend the weighing of the fleeces of the glebe sheep—Alice Dicke, Lady Laura Smart, Rose, and Cora. Later she helped with his accounts.

Her common-sense and deep sincerity made all humbug and sentiment distasteful to her, and her letters at times reveal a slight asperity that never occur in those of the others.

'Captain Pepper prosed on about "the dear men with loving hearts", and made me inclined to burst out laughing,' she wrote after an Army Charity meeting. The new curate 'is gentlemanly but does not steal our hearts away'.

Young men are generally spoken of with a mixture of raillery and patronage. There are allusions to a picnic with a young man and to subdued family excitement. Nothing came of it. I can fancy her intimidating the boy with her clear, unfaltering gaze.

Her love of animals was evidently deeply-rooted from childhood. When her pet fox escaped she roamed the woods in search of him, terrified that he might be hunted. Though so sensible with people, she was already a fool about dogs, whom she habitually pampered and over-fed. When a favourite fell ill she visited him continually through the night and dosed him heavily with castor oil and pills. On a final visit 'he sat up and begged most pitifully. I gave him bread-and-milk, which he refused—so I slipped another pill down his throat'. An hour later he died.

From her earliest years she had a keen eye for horses, and she always helped in choosing them.

Only when writing to her mother or to Mary did she throw off her habitual restraint. In a birthday letter to my grandmother she says: 'My own, my best, my dearest of mothers. We must thank our Heavenly Father for the rich gift of so sweet a mother.' To a particularly warm letter from her, Mary replies: 'Dear, dear Carry, How can I thank you for your loving words. But, dearest pet, I am not like your idea of me at all. It makes me feel very humble. Without you I should be nothing.'

This was certainly true. All her life my youngest Aunt depended on Caroline's appreciation and support. To her alone she confesses her secrets. One was her unrequited affection for a nameless young man. She has been 'guilty of a certain foolishness. But it is all over now'. The sad little letter reads as if she had recovered from an attack of measles.

Yet with all her weakness Mary appears to be the only one who felt a call to a life of wider service than Baverstock provided.

Her two elder sisters expressed amazement and guarded admiration when a young woman from a wealthy, comfortable home in their neighbourhood followed Florence Nightingale to Scutari, 'where she now stands for nine hours at the wash-tub', but felt no urge to join her. They contented themselves with collecting pennies for 'our dear gallant men in the Crimea' from the schoolchildren. But when later two acquaintances set off to start schools in Hungary Aunt Mary, now in her early twenties, questions herself anxiously. Ought not she too to be ready to give herself in a wider service than at present ? She kneels at her window to pray about it, but in the end confesses that she is too weak, too tied to the dear familiar life at home.

Caroline assures her that this furnishes her with all she
needs to ask. She settles down again to the round of cottage
visits, to teaching in the little school, to singing 'I've been
roaming, I've been roaming' (a great favourite of hers) at the
village concerts. Though no Toll Gate stood at the entrance
to Baverstock, a symbolic barrier shut out the hazardous, unknown world beyond. To pass through it required a higher
toll than any Aunt was prepared to pay.

No residence at school helped to make a breakaway easier,
for they were taught by their parents and a succession of
governesses—one of whom went off her head, and another
was found, before any damage was done, to be a Tractarian.
Even when still in the schoolroom each started to play her
part in that small, secure kingdom of Baverstock. Each had
her own families to tend and comfort, the recipients of petticoats and waistcoats of her own making, soup from special
recipes for The Working Classes and even, in particular
cases, of cream or butter from the Alderney cows. When any
sister was away news was sent of how things were going in
the cottages under her care. That all these attentions were
inspired by genuine love, as well as by a desire to do what
seemed right, to some extent checks irony.

A death in the village caused as much grief as the loss of a
favourite plant in their gardens—which is saying a good deal.
For they were passionately fond of their gardens, and, when
away on a visit, liked to hear how things were going and to
send directions to the sisters left at home.

'When you write,' begged Margaret, 'pray bestow one
word on the health of my alyssum and petunia cuttings.'
There were also directions for planting out her fuchsias and
begonias. Fuchsias, begonias, calceolarias—these continued
to be the right flowers to have all through their lives. The
Aunts invariably returned from their visits with cuttings or

seeds; to buy them was considered most extravagant. My grandmother once felt obliged to excuse herself for indulging in a whole shillingsworth of perennials to replace dead ones in an extra dry summer.

The Salisbury Flower Show was a tremendous event. 'The dear girls set off this morning each with a posy in her lap, to be put together on arrival,' wrote my grandfather. 'I should hope Margie may get first prize.'

Aunt Margaret fancied herself at flower arrangement almost as much as in the choice of clothes, which accounted perhaps for the jealousy she showed in old age when others tried to 'do the flowers'. Rightly the flowers always mattered far more than the pattern, and some of the arrangements now seen at shows would have made her sigh her soul away, as would the sight of a modern girl in jeans and pullover.

When I went to Baverstock a year or two ago I was touched on seeing, hidden in the long grass, the baulks that marked the five little separate gardens, where my Aunts had laboured so diligently for between thirty and forty years.

It was during that same visit that I met an old lady whose father remembered how, when he was a boy, my aunts took their turn at teaching in the school. They always faced their class, he said, with a little cane in one hand. He particularly remembered 'Miss Selina', standing bolt upright, as the most prompt to strike when occasion demanded. It is hard to believe that Aunt Margaret ever brought herself to strike at all; the tap would have been feather-light if she decided to give it. Sometimes, it seems, she took her sketchbook and drew portraits of the children.

One day a 'beautiful idea' flashed into her mind. She and Aunt Selina would paint the commandments in vivid colours on the church walls. This enterprise took many months to complete and gave them immense satisfaction. References to it are numerous in family letters. Into those of my grandfather, proud at first of his 'sober-minded' girls, a slight note of fretfulness creeps after a time as he expresses a hope that soon the commandments will be finished.

Through the long summer afternoons the two worked devotedly, while the squire's daughter, Vera, drove by in her pony-trap, blowing loudly on a great brass horn—all down the lane and up on to the Salisbury road. 'Is not that an *odd* thing to do?' asked Aunt Selina in a letter to her mother. Never would it have crossed their minds that perhaps the frivolous Vera thought *them* odd. None of them would knowingly have merited such an epithet.

It may have been this painting of the commandments in red and blue and gold that deepened Aunt Selina's affection for them. She always looked very cross when the vicar, in that new-fangled way of his, substituted Christ's version.

All the family shared their father's warm interest in the glebe. This is shown by the questions they ask when away from home.

'Is the clover out yet?' 'Does Mrs Muscovy sit on her eggs properly?' 'Have the sheep been shorn?' 'I can't think why the pig didn't have more than nine little ones.' All such matters were of immense importance to them.

Haymaking was the high-light of the farming year, and if any Aunt was on a visit she would chafe and fret till allowed to return. Nothing must interfere with this great event.

'Let the pony-trap meet me at Dinton,' orders my grandfather. 'I shall have only my carpet-bag and the horses will be needed in the hayfield.'

A prospect of rain brings out the whole family. 'You would have admired the field,' writes my grandmother; 'your

own six and two maids worked con amore' (my grandmother loved to use little French or Italian phrases), 'and I made them a jug of tea. Last evening appearances were alarming and we all pooked again.'

When they went to stay with their relations the Honys always took country gifts with them: a bag of choice seed potatoes, a couple of turkey eggs, two young pigs for Aunt Anne at Holton Park. 'They are much admired and Aunt is highly pleased with them,' writes a niece.

Naturally, with a life so firmly rooted in the out-door world, the letters reveal a continuous absorption with weather. My grandfather kept a log-book recording the wind, the temperature, the rainfall.

'Look to the rainfall,' he writes to Aunt Caroline, 'and let it be set down carefully as it will be something remarkable.'

I can see Aunt Carry leaving her place at the breakfast table and hastening to the garden as it struck nine—just as my father used to run out with a cry of: 'It's raining into yesterday!'

Many admonitions are given against exposure to the east wind, but the west wind 'brings comfort and delicious feelings'. Thunder-storms weighed heavily on both spirits and head, particularly on those of my grandmother and Aunt Margaret. They were alike, too, in the delight they drew from gazing at the sky.

'The clouds seemed charged with black snow, so dense and dark they were.' 'This is the day there was to be a *black* rainbow. . . In Salisbury there was quite a commotion about it.'

'Venus was in full beauty just opposite my window. Jupiter is admiring her on one side and Mars on the other. No marvel she is vain.' Such were among the innumerable comments in their letters. Unfortunately Venus, the black rainbow, Aunt Margaret's comet and aurora are all outweighed by wildness and wetness; by 'A mizzling rain, disagreeable beyond description'; by cruel snow and frost in May; by east winds that bring colds and sore throats and discomfort. In my grandmother's diary for November 1839 I found these entries. 'Common routine. I cannot get out because of the rain. Time stealing gently on.' 'Ditto, ditto' follows. Then comes a break. 'The sun shines. Let us appreciate its beauteous beams.'

Beyond the garden and the glebe the place dearest to my Aunts was Groveley Wood, set on a hillside a mile or so north of their home. For them it was enchanted ground, and as I read of their affection for it I remembered the low intense voice which Aunt Margaret used whenever she spoke of it. In the Wood grew the sweetest white violets in all England; the finest hazels; its nightingales were the most musical. The villagers, too, appreciated the Wood and swarmed there to pick the nuts: once my grandfather found all the cottages empty on a fine September afternoon because everyone was nutting (and small wonder since low wages could be supplemented by selling the result at 12s. a sack). But for the nightingales there was no competition and my Aunts could enjoy their kingdom undisturbed on May evenings. Never can there have been so many allusions to nightingales in any collection of letters.

'We enjoyed a full concert for over half-an-hour. It was delicious.' 'Alas, during this cruel May the nightingales have

remained silent. I suppose the cold weather has given them sore throats.' Once, however: 'a brave fellow sang during a snow storm.' So it goes on. As the evening mists rose my Aunts crept silently away, because these were dangerous and the birds must not be disturbed. Sometimes one sang in the churchyard, or on the pear tree as the Aunts dug in their gardens.

From abroad, Aunt Margaret writes characteristically: 'Give my love to the dear nightingales. It is so good of them to come to us.'

Now, I realized better what memories haunted my Aunts when they stood in wrapt silence under the oak at Eling to listen to a nightingale.

That the larks, pouring out their songs above the downs just outside Groveley, never commanded the same romantic affection is proved by a horrid item in my grandmother's account book: 'Paid for 1 doz. larks . . . 1s.'

Skating provided a robuster occupation for everyone but Aunt Margaret, whose fragile body evidently shrank from contact with hard ice. Stout-hearted Aunt Caroline writes: 'The bishop's daughter pushed into me and caused me a severe fall, which shook my courage very much.' As children they used to hurry off to Dinton pond, while their poor brother looked on from his wheeled chair. Later they went further afield to Clarendon Park, where no doubt their grandmother, Selina Byam, had watched the gentlemen showing themselves off to advantage when she was young. Her own clothes would have made it impossible for her to join them even had it been considered proper to do so, and my Aunts and their friends were still also absurdly handicapped by long, inflated skirts.

'Never shall I forget Mary Jacob sitting in an inch of water with her foot through her hoops,' wrote my father.

When they were young as well as when they were old, tea parties played an important part in my Aunts' lives. They drove out, two at a time in the pony-cart or behind a pair of donkeys, to visit their friends and sometimes remained till next morning.

'Margie and Linnie drank tea at Compton and stayed the night,' wrote their mother. 'Louie, whose turn it was to go, had a cut on her nose which does not unite properly.' It must have been a sad disappointment for Louisa had a passion for outings of all sorts. It is to be noted that when invitations came it was the established rule that Aunt Selina, as the eldest, must always be consulted first.

Later on tea parties grew more exciting. 'Only fancy!' exclaimed Great Aunt Caroline. 'King Croquet has arrived in Bath!' This was in 1850. Soon the click of mallets sounded in most large gardens in southern England. From Dorset Aunt Mary wrote: 'The Saunders took us to a large, grand croquet party at Fleet House. I was very glad of my Algerian silk as people like to look smart. . . It was very pleasant . . . ices, claret and cider cup and tea, and then a cold collation with champaign at 7 o'clock.'

As I have said their peaceful life at Baverstock was constantly broken by visits to aunts. These differed profoundly from our own in one respect. We were fussed over and made much of, and were inclined to take all the kindness heaped on us very much for granted. But our own Aunts usually went to tend and comfort, and often received more pain than pleasure.

'Aunt Henrietta is *not* comfortable to be with, never cosy —trying to be kind but always contradictory and opposed to everything one does,' or again: 'Aunt is a little *crooked* this morning, but I took no notice and sat playing my fiddle upstairs.' 'Aunt Selina is now so engrossed with herself' (strange how similarity of name went with similarity of character since this was the complaint constantly made against our own Aunt Selina), 'and her peculiar view of things has increased, so that she does *not* contribute to the happiness of others'.

'But dear Aunt Carry is the soul of Christianity.' Just as she had been my grandfather's favourite sister, she remained the favourite aunt.

Aunt Anne developed into a formidable lady who exhausted her nieces and herself with her restless energy. No longer did 'time flow on in such pleasing serenity for her that she scarcely realized that evening had come', as her sister wrote of her once. She asked too many questions and continually changed her mind. When they drove out behind a young pony, 'she was quite beside herself,' wrote Aunt Margaret, 'and the coachman terrified because one moment she shouted to him to drive on and the next moment to stop. She looked so excited that I could hardly keep from laughing, and then I felt I was going to cry.' Another time she forced both husband and niece to accompany her in an open carriage though 'it was *so* cold. Uncle and I both suffered', complained Aunt Margaret. 'In the evening she grew very lively but I had a toothache and felt rather cross.' Yet always Aunt Margaret's conscience smote her after such strictures. 'I know Aunt is kind at bottom, but the outward crust is a sort of irritation. . . But when I think of all my faults so lovingly forgiven at home tears blind my eyes.'

Her sister Mary, aged sixteen, however, writes unrepentantly of Aunt Anne's vagaries. When seven ladies were due to dine she was ordered to sup alone upstairs, but then, as they streamed into the house, 'aunt became so flustered that she sent word for me to tidy myself and come down at once.' Mary revenges herself by adding: 'Aunt did *not* look well. She is too old to wear a low dress, all white satin and silk.'

Aunt Anne's parsimony over coal was another trial. Fires were postponed till the last possible moment, and even then she would 'follow the maid from room to room seeing that not a lump too much was used'. A niece, her hands covered by chilblains, lamented how cold it was—and how stuffy. No window might be opened. I remembered how we used to suffocate in the Blue Room, and how we crept from our bed to let in a little air when Aunt Louisa had left us.

During widowhood and old age Aunt Anne grew increasingly demanding and difficult. A niece must come posthaste when needed, must walk beside her donkey-chair, fall in with every whim. Also the old lady took to sending odd, untidy, embarrassing little parcels by rail—oranges, a few broken biscuits, cast-off clothes.

'From the torn paper,' writes Aunt Margaret, 'an old lace mantle unfolded itself. . . Aunt used to look nice in it, but now it is flimsy and dusty and in out-moded fashion. But perhaps it is still beautiful to her, so I must not hurt her feelings.'

And I remembered regretfully how bluntly I had refused a black corded silk coat with a ruffle at the neck, 'to wear when you go motoring with your husband'. I should have accepted it gracefully and consigned it to the dressing-up box.

In what my Aunts endured a pattern was repeating itself, for in her youth Aunt Anne had suffered in just the same way from her own Aunt Anne. 'Yes, my love,' my grandmother wrote to her, 'it is indeed trying to gaze on decayed faculties.'

Unfortunately my Aunts' troublesome old relative continued to eat with zest and took a long time to die. Other old aunts, too, needed attention, though none so much as Aunt Anne.

Compared with aunts, their Uncle Peter worried his nieces very little, though he startled them unceasingly by the way he roamed from place to place.

'Peter is an *extraordinary* person to do so much at his age,' wrote my grandfather in 1849. 'I hope he will not overdo it but will take his repose at Seville.' Peter lived twenty-seven years after that and continued taking his repose everywhere. He was always much concerned about his health, consulted

doctors all over Europe, and sometimes passed on their pre-
scriptions. A Neapolitan dentist advised 'a Turkey fig or two
boiled in sweet milk', and a Paris physician recommended
White Mustard for a variety of complaints. Margie had
better try it for her Bile. He favoured Baverstock with an
immense number of letters retailing the latest gossip and
commenting on public affairs, and particularly on the state
of 'the Funds'.

When he ceased to wander so far afield he occasionally
honoured his brother with a visit and distressed the family
by his resolute refusal to take exercise. But Aunt Carry recorded that once when the cook fell ill and she told him there
would be no dinner unless someone fetched it from a neighbouring farm 'he ran like a partridge in the rain'.

Despite their penalties, these earlier auntly visits brought
many pleasures, as did those of our generation to Eling.
There were the Ascot days and trips to London—though
these were sometimes spoiled by Aunt Anne's habit of keeping them sitting in her cab while she paid her bills and then
giving them sandwiches from her bag instead of a meal at
one of the smart new restaurants. On the other hand, she took
Aunt Margaret to the Royal Academy, where she gazed
with deep emotion at Landseer's 'Stag Pursued by Hounds'
across a lake and at 'Lee's magnificent picture of two
gigantic waves'.

Also they walked in Kensington Gardens and saw
Waterer's 'wondrous rhododendrons', and Margaret, accompanied by the maid, was allowed to buy herself a new mantle
at Cavendish House, while Louisa slipped into Fortnum's
for half a pound of dried turtle. The only trouble was the
appalling mud and the fact that in London they could not
wear their treasured goloshes.

Naturally the high-light of all London visits was one to

the Great Exhibition, where the Aunts dipped their hand-kerchiefs in the Eau-de-Cologne Fountain.

Even at Wokingham there were compensations. The day after Aunt Mary had helped entertain the seven ladies at dinner: 'Aunt was in high good humour and allowed the coachman to drive me after the stag-hounds in a high light cart over plowed fields and at such a pace!'

Aunt Selina was sent to stay with her grandmother and her three aunts at Bath to drink the waters, but she thought them 'abominable' and begged to come home. Her mother told her she 'should be grateful for them to her Heavenly Father', but this was too much even for Aunt Selina's piety.

A real adventure was a driving tour in Wales which Aunt Margaret and Aunt Caroline took with their Aunt Anne. Of course it was a mixed joy because 'Aunt does not fancy any of the places so far, and is beginning to wonder why she brought all the luggage and servants about with so much expense'. The inn at Festiniog was dirty, Dolgelly too noisy; always something was wrong. But the girls were thrilled to climb part of the way up Cader Idris with a little boy as guide, to watch the market crowd in Llangollen and the women in their scarlet cloaks and steeple hats, and to learn for themselves a few sentences of this 'strange and musical language'.

When staying at Ryde in the spring of 1854 Aunt Carry was taken by her Aunt Caroline to see 'our brave Queen leading forth her Fleet as far as the Nab. . . It is said she suffers extremely.'

So in the end the pleasanter and more exciting memories prevailed, and when one of the Aunts died, 'the dear girls desire to have a little hair reserved for them,' wrote my grandmother. They remembered the gay days at Ascot, the trips to London, the sunrise at Sark, the towering Welsh mountains, the ships sailing for the Crimea, the gallop across ploughed fields, and forgot the discomforts and irritations.

And when I finished the letters I found myself recalling not so much the Aunts' odd ways and all the fussiness so at variance with our life at home, as the happy things: the hallowed smell and twilight in the Round House; the rainbow balls; trotting on Tommy through the Manor Woods; picnicking beside Southampton Water; watching the Fleet lit up by thousands of brilliant-coloured lights for Queen Victoria's Diamond Jubilee. All these and a hundred others sprang to life again.

And the Baverstock letters took me back to the Honys' earthly paradise, up the lane to Groveley, and then to the double row of long grey tombstones under which lay Aunts and great-aunts and great-grandmother, as well as grandfather and grandmother. An old man told me that try as he would he could not keep the mould from gathering on the stones. A robin was singing but no nightingale.

But my Aunts were not there. They were hay-making in the vicarage field, or hurrying in their pink and blue delaine gowns to the wood; entering the church with dedicated faces and pots of paint; or sweeping to and fro, armed with bows and arrows, across the lawns of Wilton.